# LOOKING FOR JESUS

Meditations on the Last Discourse
of St. John

By

Adrian van Kaam, C.S.Sp.

DIMENSION BOOKS, INC.

Denville, New Jersey

# BOOKS BY THE AUTHOR

*A Light to the Gentiles*
*Religion and Personality*
*Personality Fulfillment in the Spiritual Life*
*Existential Foundations of Psychology*
*The Art of Existential Counseling*
*The Demon and the Dove* [co-author]
*Personality Fulfillment in the Religious Life*
*The Vowed Life*
*The Emergent Self* [co-author]
*The Participant Self* [co-author]
*On Being Involved*
*Envy and Originality*
*On Being Yourself*
*Spirituality and the Gentle Life*
*In Search of Spiritual Identity*
*The Dynamics of Spiritual Self Direction*
*The Woman at the Well*
*Tell Me Who I am* [co-author]
*Looking for Jesus*

# LOOKING FOR JESUS

Meditations on the Last Discourse of St. John

By

ADRIAN VAN KAAM, C.S.Sp.

DIMENSION BOOKS, INC.
Denville, New Jersey

FIRST AMERICAN EDITION BY
DIMENSION BOOKS INC.

L.C.C.C. No. 77-93534
I.S.B.N. 0-87193-064-1


**Imprimi Potest:** *Rev. Philip J. Haggerty, C.S.Sp.
Provincial*

**Nihil Obstat:** *Rev. William J. Winter, S.T.D. Censor
Librorum*

**Imprimatur:** *Most Rev. Vincent M. Leonard, D.D.
Bishop of Pittsburgh*

November 10, 1977

# TABLE OF CONTENTS

## FOREWORD

This book is not an exegetical commentary; it is a book of scriptural meditations written from the perspective of formative spirituality.

The author—in accordance with the principles of this new religious discipline—takes into account the doctrine of the Church and the main information gained from exegesis and from scriptural and systematic theology. This approach could be compared to that of architecture and engineering both of which imply the use of the axioms and findings of mathematics, or to the discipline of education which builds on some basic insights of psychology and philosophy.

The student of formative spirituality goes beyond this basis of doctrine and exegetical-theological information on which he ecessarily builds. He asks himself what kind of meditative reading of the scriptures might effectively foster the formation of the personal-spiritual life of the reader in the light of the Holy Spirit. The Fathers of the Church, the Desert Fathers, and the great spiritual masters have given us over the centuries numerous examples of such post-exegetical meditative readings of the scriptures in service of the unfolding of the interiority of the Christian.

This inspirational-practical approach has been applied here to the first part of the last discourse of Jesus in the Gospel of St. John. It is a sequel to *The Woman at the Well,* a first attempt by the author to apply the principles of formative spirituality to selected passages of St. John's gospel.

Some readers may be interested in the approach of formative spirituality to scripture reading as one of the basic exercises of the Christian in search of his life form in Christ. The Epilogue at the end of this book has been written to meet their interest. This Epilogue is a sequel to the Epilogue in *The Woman at the Well* and to two chapters about the same approach that can be found respectively in the author's books: *In Search of Spiritual Identity* and *The Dynamics of Spiritual Self Direction.*

May the Holy Spirit grace author and readers with his light, for without him all words are like chaff in the wind.

## ACKNOWLEDGMENTS

I am very grateful to the Academic Program Coordinator and Assistant Director of the Center for the Study of Spirituality at the Institute of Man, Susan Annette Muto, Ph.D., and to Mrs. Otis Carney, both of whom offered me many criticisms and suggestions that were influential in the final editing of this book. I thank the office personnel of the Institute, especially the secretary, Ms. Collette McIntyre, Mrs. William Harris and Mrs. Robert Littlefield for their generous typing and proofreading of the manuscript and the many other chores that accompany the preparation of a publication.

# I

## JESUS' FAREWELL TO HIS FOLLOWERS

As soon as Judas had taken the piece of bread he
went out. Night had fallen.

When he had gone Jesus said:


"Now has the Son of Man been glorified,
and in him God has been glorified.
If God has been glorified in him,
God will in turn glorify him in himself,
and will glorify him very soon.

"My little children,
I shall not be with you much longer.
You will look for me,
and, as I told the Jews,
where I am going,
you cannot come.
I give you a new commandment:
love one another:
just as I have loved you,
you also must love one another.
By this love you have for one another,
everyone will know that you are my disciples."

Simon Peter said, "Lord, where are you going?" Jesus replied, "Where I am going you cannot follow me now; you will follow me later." Peter said to him, "Why can't I follow you now? I will lay down my life for you." "Lay down your life for me?" answered Jesus. "I tell you most solemnly, before the cock crows you will have disowned me three times.

(Jn. 13:30-38)

"Do not let your hearts be troubled.
Trust in God still, and trust in me.
There are many rooms in my Father's house;
if there were not, I should have told you.
I am going now to prepare a place for you,
and after I have gone and prepared you a place,
I shall return to take you with me;
so that where I am
you may be too.
You know the way to the place where I am going."

Thomas said, "Lord, we do not know where you are going, so how can we know the way? Jesus said:

"I am the Way, the Truth and the Life.
No one can come to the Father except through me.
If you know me, you know my Father too.
From this moment you know him and have seen him."

Philip said, "Lord, let us see the Father and then we shall be satisfied." "Have I been with you all this time, Philip," said Jesus to him, "and you still do not know me?"

"To have seen me is to have seen the Father,
so how can you say, 'Let us see the Father?'
Do you not believe
that I am in the Father and the Father is in me?
The words I say to you I do not speak as from myself:
it is the Father, living in me, who is doing this work.
You must believe me when I say
that I am in the Father and the Father is in me;
believe it on the evidence of this work, if for no other
reason.
I tell you solemnly,
whoever believes in me
will perform the same works as I do myself,
he will perform even greater works,
because I am going to the Father.
Whatever you ask for in my name I will do,
so that the Father may be glorified in the Son.
If you ask for anything in my name,
I will do it.
If you love me you will keep my commandments.
I shall ask the Father,
and he will give you another Advocate
to be with you for ever,
that Spirit of truth
whom the world can never receive
since it neither sees nor knows him;
but you know him,
because he is with you, he is in you.
I will not leave you orphans;
I will come back to you.
In a short time the world will no longer see me;
but you will see me,
because I live and you will live.
On that day
you will understand that I am in my Father
and you in me and I in you.          (John 14:19-20)

Anybody who receives my commandments and keeps them
will be one who loves me;
and anybody who loves me will be loved by my Father,
and I shall love him and show myself to him."

Judas—this was not Judas Iscariot—said to him
"Lord, what is all this about? Do you intend to show
yourself to us and not to the world?" Jesus replied:

"If anyone loves me he will keep my word,
and my Father will love him,
and we shall come to him
and make our home with him.
Those who do not love me do not keep my words.
And my word is not my own:
it is the word of the one who sent me.
I have said these things to you
while still with you;
but the Advocate, the Holy Spirit,
whom the Father will send in my name,
will teach you everything
and remind you of all I have said to you.
Peace I bequeath to you,
my own peace I give you,
a peace the world cannot give, this is my gift to you.
Do not let your hearts be troubled or afraid.
You heard me say:
I am going away, and shall return.
If you loved me you would have been glad to know that I am
going to the father,
for the Father is greater than I.
I have told you this now before it happens,
so that when it does happen you may believe.
I shall not talk with you any longer,
because the prince of this world is on his way.

He has no power over me,
but the world must be brought to know that I love the Father
and that I am doing exactly what the Father told me.
Come now, let us go.

(Jn. 14:1-31)

The farewell words of our Lord inspired John to compose some of the most spiritual pages ever written. They have been an inspiration for Christians of all ages. Commented upon by scholars and saints, their richness will never be exhausted. Mystics and people of simple prayer have been nourished by this discourse; we too are invited to live these words to the full.

Jesus' talk on the new life enlightens the mind while touching the heart. It is a testimony of mysterious depth that brings comfort and consolation—words that have changed the lives of countless people. No wonder that on his deathbed St. Francis begged his friars to read to him slowly these words of Jesus. To hear them was his last consolation.

This discourse complements the Sermon on the Mount. In that sermon, given at the beginning of his active life, Jesus taught us a new morality: the sublime message of the beatitudes. His words at the last supper tell us about the inner life itself of God and the Christian; they describe our oneness with the Father and the Spirit in Jesus. They speak about an intimacy with the Divine unheard of before. These words are the ultimate source for any spirituality of the Kingdom for all centuries to come, to be embraced by all cultures.

John pictures our Lord speaking to the sad, silent men around him. He gathers all he remembers of Jesus' sayings about the spiritual life. During a life of prayer and contemplation, the deepest meaning of these words has been disclosed to this disciple. He now senses what his Master meant. He brings this whole message together in the farewell discourse at the end of the Lord's life so that we too may dwell on it; he intends us to read it as the final words of a beloved friend who left us with a lasting mission.

The farewell of the Master is meditated upon by John under the infallible guidance of the Spirit; it is Jesus' goodbye to those who are truly his in the world while not being of the world. He sees his disciples in the world as orphans bewildered and alone, their hearts heavy with fear. Jesus enshrines here his tenderness and compassion. His words touch the core of our lives.

Judas has just left the room to betray him. Jesus is alone with his friends. He wants to tell them about his own inner life, to help them see how they can live it themselves when he is no longer bodily with them. They would not be able to grasp all of it, but they might remember later what he is trying to communicate at this moment. Their human spirit will then be enlightened by the Holy Spirit, who will remind them of these words. He will teach them everything Jesus meant to impress on them. John, the disciple he loves, will carry these words in his heart, savoring them for a lifetime.

John will later compare these words with other sayings of Jesus. This comparison enables him to bring together in one discourse Jesus' message about the spiritual life.

Though Jesus' words are tinged with sadness, the light of hope is in them. We sense elation about his victory over death, about the manifestation of the glory of God to be released in humanity.

Many readers of these last words of our Lord have told us what their most meaningful message was for them.

For some it was the new commandment: to love one another as Jesus loved them. (Jn. 13:34) For others it was the role the words of Jesus should play in their lives. (Jn. 14:21, 23; 17:6) Some were touched by his promise of the Spirit and what this would mean in the life of the faithful. (Jn. 14:16-18) Still others were inspired by his telling them how at one they should be with him, with the Father and the Spirit dwelling within them. (Jn. 14:20-21, 23-24; 17:21)

Each of these experiences, evoked by Jesus' words, can be genuine for the Christian. We too may ask ourselves what this reading can teach us about the unique life form God wants for us? How does the spirituality of Jesus differ from spiritualities that develop today and from those that originated before the Eternal Word assumed our humanity? You and I, together with our fellow Christians over the centuries, are called to live the life of Jesus between his departure and return.

This farewell of Jesus contains answers to our deepest questions: How can I live in and with Jesus after he bodily has left the earth? How can I be faithful to the life of the Spirit in a world so often at odds with his love? What may I hope for when I open myself to his presence? How does Jesus abide in me? How can I cope with pain and fear and still witness for my Lord? How do I share the life of the followers of Jesus all over the earth?

The answers of Jesus to these questions are eternally new. The Incarnate Word, entering into our history, initiated a new spirituality, one that goes infinitely beyond any other no matter how impressive it may be. Pre-Christian spiritualities are rooted in an experience of oneness with nature and with mystery that penetrates and goes beyond people and their world, but lack the revelation of the personal core of that mystery, the life of the Trinity and of our calling to share it.

The spirituality of Jesus differs from that of the old covenant. The latter was built on a revelation of God as the ruling yet loving King of Creation.

The new spirituality of Jesus does not exclude these older forms; it presupposes and complements them. In his last discourse Jesus adds an unheard-of dimension to the already existing ways of union with the Divine: an intimate sharing in the inner life itself of the Godhead. He tells us how to receive, expand and protect that intimacy.

The new life will be marked by oneness with the Risen Lord. He is more than ever present to us who surrender to him, but now in the Spirit. He will be more alive in us than he was in his disciples during his scant three years with them. He will be active in us through his Spirit, who, as he tells us in the farewell, will transform our spirit.

What really happens here is that Jesus creates a new space, a new world of spiritual meaning in which his followers can live. He offers nourishment for a Christ-like existence in the midst of a world they are called to transform gently and slowly over the millenia. This existence, as Jesus explains, will be rooted in faithfulness to his word and his love.

John gathered in the first twelve chapters of his Gospel all the deeds and words of Jesus that could lead unbelievers to believe in him. Here at the end he wants to bring together Jesus' message for those who not only believe but who want to deepen their faith to a life of union with him.

This discourse is John's synthesis of a Christian spirituality; it offers a climax at the end of his Gospel flowing from life-long meditations on all he remembers the Lord ever said about the life of intimacy with him. He combines these sayings of the Lord with his final words at a dramatic last moment of intimacy with his disciples before his passion and death. Poised between time and eternity, Jesus speaks as still living on earth and yet as being already beyond it.

Jesus makes us feel that you and I, that all of us, are in his mind when he says,

"I pray not only for these,
but for those also
who through their words will believe in me."

(Jn. 17:20)

Dwelling on these texts, we must be deeply aware of this attention of Jesus to us. Imagine yourself behind the listening faces of these sad fishermen, hidden in the shadows thrown by the flickering lights of oil lamps. In the shadow of their faces are all the faces of mankind. You and I are there; Christ speaks to us. Imagine him looking right at you and speaking these words. Ponder his divinity, radiated into this simple room, where he speaks of the glory the Father has given him before the foundation of the world. Sense the warmth and sadness, the elation and suffering of his humanity. Love him for himself and for his care of you. When the Spirit graces you with this gift of presence to his words, let yourself be touched by this most sublime spiritual teaching of all ages.

John places Jesus' discourse in the setting of the last meal he enjoyed with his disciples, the passover meal of the Jews. Such a celebration was an occasion for people to take their food in the style of the Romans. A low table was set up. The table had three sides occupied by the guests taking the festive meal; one side was kept free to enable the servants to serve quietly and swiftly. The guests did not sit on chairs. They would recline on mats or couches. The table had to be low. Not having the backs and arms of chairs to sustain them, they would support themselves on their left elbow keeping their right arm and hand free for eating and drinking.

Jesus delays his last discourse until he has given Judas leave to betray him.

As soon as Judas had taken the piece of bread he
went out. Night had fallen. (Jn. 13:30)

Outside the lamp-lighted cenacle, darkness had fallen on Jerusalem. This darkness reminds us of John's words in the beginning of his Gospel. He speaks there about the life Jesus came to bring us. "That life", he says, "was the light of men, a light that shines in the dark, a light that darkness could not overpower." (Jn. 1:4-5)

Judas had chosen to stay in the darkness of spirit in which all humans are born since the fall of man. The light of Jesus had shone upon him, as it had on the other apostles, but for him it had been in vain. He preferred darkness because his deeds were evil. (Jn. 3:19) Yet that darkness could not overpower the light of Jesus; after Judas' betrayal it would begin to shine forth in the world and penetrate all history.

The phrase "Night had fallen" reminds us also of the darkness that would make it impossible for Jesus to keep preaching the new tidings:

"As long as the day lasts
I must carry out the work of the one who sent me;
the night will soon be here when no one can work."

(Jn. 9:4)

Judas had been gently dismissed by Jesus to leave for an errand in the city. Freely, in equanimity before his Father, Jesus allows him to go to initiate the final act of the drama of salvation. Leaving Jesus, the light of the world, brings night to the soul of Judas. As St. Augustine says, the man who went out into the night had become night himself.

The faithful remnant of the disciples, who were open to the light, remained with Jesus in the solitude of the cenacle. All the attention of Jesus is now directed towards his Father in heaven and towards this little band of followers of the light given to him by his Father. (Jn. 17:6) Judas has already cut himself off; he has left the circle of trusted friends. Jesus can now open his heart to them, withholding nothing.

# II

## CHILDHOOD AND SPIRITUALITY

"My little children,
I shall not be with you much longer.
You will look for me,
and, as I told the Jews,
where I am going,
you cannot come." (Jn. 13:33-34)


Each Gospel expresses the personal faith experience of the New Testament writers. Each of them presents his experience of Jesus in his own way. St. John too tells how he felt about the Lord, what his words and deeds meant to him. He lets us share in his own spirituality. If I enter into John's experience, it may become for me a source of illumination and enrichment.

In these words of the discourse, Jesus begins to speak to "his own" about his leaving them. It is a shocking announcement, but he consoles his friends with the promise that his leaving will not be the end of his presence among them. It will be the beginning of a whole new kind of indwelling in humanity and history.

His life will become ours in a mysterious way. We will be able to live with Jesus' own life. We will share his interiority. This sharing of life will relieve the anguish of his disciples by a grace of intimacy undreamt of before. He will permeate similarly the lives of all believers; we will be in communion with one another all over the globe and all through history: a shared life in the indwelling Lord.

Jesus calls them, "My little children," an address that did not sound strange in this setting. The last supper was the Passover meal. Usually it was celebrated in a family. A significant part of the ceremony was the father's explanation of the meaning of the meal to the children around the table. Any group of Jewish believers coming together for the Passover meal—like Jesus and his apostles—would more or less behave as if they were in a family. The person presiding would act like a father.

The words, "My little children," show Jesus' compassion, his awareness of their vulnerability. He does not address them as a powerful coach would a rugged team of players; he does not give them a pep talk: Be above sentiment! Take my leaving unflinchingly! He wants to let them know that he really feels what they are feeling, that he is well aware what a disillusion his defeat will be for them. They had left everything, their homes, jobs, and families, to follow him. They enjoyed his company for only a few years. They love and revere him. They think the world of him. They dream and brag among themselves about their promising future when he will have arisen to greatness in a liberated Israel. They are already bickering with one another about who should have the highest positions. He had become the whole meaning of their lives. And now he has to tell them that he is going away, that he will not be with them much longer.

He knows how it will hurt them, how they will be looking for him in vain, how their lives will be broken, their dreams destroyed, how they will be at a loss about what to do, where to go. Hence this note of care: "My little children."

In the face of Jesus' gentleness, I feel embarrassed by my abruptness. How often do I bring people unpleasant tidings without delicacy and compassion. Rarely do I take time to put myself in their place. I do not really try to feel what they are feeling. I give it to them straight, secretly proud of my no-nonsense approach. I harden my heart and become less like him who lovingly dwells in me.

"Lord, grant me your gentleness. Your sensitivity for pain in my fellow men. Your respect for weakness and vulnerability. Make me a new creation. Let your Spirit inspire words of compassion that lessen suffering, words that show to people that I am their companion on the road of affliction and distress, words that let the gift of divine love flow out toward others in need of sympathy.

"Your words, 'My little children,' fill my soul with consolation. You know how vulnerable I am. You care for me like a mother for her child. You often conceal your solicitude, but it is always there. Your hidden compassion carries me through dreary days even if I don't feel your presence. At such moments it is as if you repeat to me: 'I shall not be with you much longer. You will look for me in vain.' You warn me that you will leave me so that I will not be more attached to your consolation than to you."

We are always children. We are only slowly emerging to the maturity of our unique self in Jesus. The fullness of perfection will only be granted to us when we enter eternity. In this sense, we are always children here on earth.

We are also children in a deeper and everlasting sense. To be a child before God is our essential condition. The deepest meaning of childhood is at the basis of our spiritual life.

"It is good to be a child, my Lord. For, as a child, you called me by a name of my own. I am never merely a case for you among other cases. A child has a deep personal meaning for his parents; he is cared for as the most important treasure in their life. I too am held uniquely in the attention of your Father. A child relaxes in the embrace of his mother. I should relax, too, for I am embraced by the mystery that cares for me. Your loving attention never pauses no matter how far I go astray. To be a child at heart is to entrust myself to your caring presence. To be a child before you is to accept my finitude, to love my limitation, to confess that life is a mystery I cannot preside over by any power of my own."

Childhood is a peaceful knowing that God's love endures in spite of my aberration. Sinfulness is in me from the beginning of my life. I am born in the midst of a history already wrought before me, a history of shared human guilt, of resistance to the call of the Eternal. Original sin makes me vulnerable from the beginning; also, in that sense, I am a little child. I can only survive by the embrace of the Eternal who shelters and sanctifies me.

"To be a child before you is to see my guilt within the greater grace and compassion of you, my Lord. A child feels safe in the love and protection of those who are stronger and wiser than he. If I stand in this experience of childlike deficiency before you, the Father will shield me.

"To be a little child is to be delivered over to the mystery of Providence. Make me guileless and serene as children are. Let me live in the simple faith that what you allow to happen to me is always for the best. For only a childlike spirit can experience your presence as sheltering and forgiving."

Childhood is one of the fundamentals of the Christian life. It personifies trust, relaxed openness, wonder, docility, a serene flowing with the unpredictable. A childlike sense of trust and wonder, of eager docility, should animate us. Then we journey into the unknown and the unexpected with eyes wide open with delight like little children at the Father's hand.

What else is spiritual childhood than the enactment of the basic attitudes of the spirit: faith, hope, and love. As long as we are like children, we are on the right path. We go forward in the measure that we allow this childhood to unfold. The essence of childhood is openness. We must maintain that openness despite experiences that tend to close us. Such openness to the infinite can only be a gift of God. Without grace it would be impossible to acquire or maintain. We are called to Divine Sonship in the Son. Jesus, as Divine Word, is eternally generated by the Father. His is an eternal divine childhood. We are invited to share in his divine childhood by grace.

To live spiritually is to preserve the spirit of childhood within myself, to regain it when it is lost, to restore its power when it is weakened. The opposite is pride. "Every proud man is an abomination to the Lord; I assure you that he will not go unpunished." (Pv. 16:5) His punishment is the loss of wonder and openness, of the sense of adventure that is the salt of life and love.

## III

## LOOKING FOR JESUS

"You will look for me" (Jn. 13:33)

Remember how eagerly you looked out the window as a child when your Mother told you that Daddy would be back from a long trip abroad with stories, gifts, surprises. You had missed him so much; now this afternoon, this evening, he will be back. You sat anxiously at the window, your little nose pressed against the cold pane of glass, staring intently at the people passing in the street.

Looking is not seeing. It is a wanting, a trying to see. How badly you wanted your Dad to show up among all these passersby.

Looking is patient and recollected. It gives up all things that interfere with loving vigilance. You stayed at the window, forgot about your play, your friends, your toys, the good-smelling things Mother was preparing in the kitchen . . . Dad may be coming any moment now, I should not miss him.

Looking is loving. Every time you thought you recognized him in that figure still far away—"that may be he"—your heart beat faster.

Looking is believing and hoping. No matter how often you were disappointed—"Again that's not he"—you kept growing in hope: maybe he is the next one or perhaps the person after that.

Looking is suffering in love. Time passed by, the sky darkened, the lights went on. You felt the strain in your eyes, your empty tummy, the stiffness in your body. And yet you lived in the faith and hope: he may be here any moment now. You did not mind all these things; you only wanted to be at hand the instant Daddy would show his face, swing open the door and embrace you.

While looking for him, your expectation, your faith, your love kept growing, filling your heart abundantly. Is this not an image of what looking for Jesus can do for our soul?

How many splendid tales are told about lovers who grew in their love by looking for the beloved far away. The lonely soldier or traveler taking off for war or for a foreign land filled with dangers was buoyed up and carried by the joyful persuasion: one person eagerly awaits my safe return.

Think about the classic story in the *Odyssey*. Penelope, the wife of Odysseus, was "looking for him". Her husband had gone off with others fearlessly to besiege Troy. She had promised to keep looking for him in daily faithfulness.

Troy had fallen. Odysseus did not return. A long and arduous voyage kept him far away from her. But Penelope kept looking for him in love and longing.

Many chieftains of Ithaca and the islands round about became her suitors, begging her to give up her desperate looking for Odysseus. To justify that foolish vigilance, to rid herself of their importunities, she bade them to allow her to keep looking for his arrival until she had woven a winding sheet for old Laertes, the father of Odysseus. But every night she undid the piece that she had woven by day. A stratagem of love and looking. This she did for three long years of daily watching for a ship that might bring Odysseus home. And finally he came, delighted by a wife who had grown deeply in her love because of her looking and longing in fidelity.

What happened to her growth in love happens infinitely more to the soul who looks for Jesus who seems far away. He knows that we are looking for him in fidelity; this pleases him and he fills our souls with graces we do not suspect in our loneliness.

> "You will look for me,
> and, as I told the Jews,
> where I am going
> you cannot come."    (Jn. 13:33-34)

Often Jesus will hide himself from our eyes. Our hearts feel cold and stony. He seems farther away than Odysseus ever was. Without him, our daily task feels like the weaving of a useless piece of winding sheet that we undo every night, waiting desperately for him alone. We are looking for the Lord, but our hearts are pained, for the Lord withholds himself. We realize that we cannot come where he really is. He is Emmanuel: God with us. But God is ineffable mystery, known only in a cloud of unknowing.

My Lord reveals and conceals himself in a life-long mystery of divine "hide and seek". Any thought, feeling, image I may have about Jesus tells me something about him but hides infinitely more. Any image is limited; it is always immeasurably less than the fullness of his glory. The only manner in which Jesus can make me grow towards him as he really is, is the way of revealing and concealing.

At times, he gives himself to me, to encourage me on the way, to comfort me in my weakness and solitude, to relieve the pain of longing, the suffering of searching. It is the springtime of inner revelation, filled with the joy of finding him again. When my beloved feels I have become strong enough to bear with further growth in the life of union with Mystery, he warns me softly:

*I shall not be with you much longer. I have given you the grace not to forget me when I take leave of you. It is good for you that I go, but believe me I will be present to you in my absence. You will look for me with love and longing. There will be many suitors claiming your heart. Be faithful and your pained longing will purify your presence to me. Your love will become more a love of the spirit, less a love of the flesh. You will realize humbly that where I have gone you cannot come, that your mind cannot capture the fullness of the mystery of my divinity. Your growing love and longing will reach further than your mind could. Yet even your ardent love does not go so far as to exhaust the mystery of my Divinity. I shall withdraw from you because I love you. I desire so much to lift you beyond the limited image of me that begins to mean too much for you.*

*In my own good time I shall return to the dried-up garden of your soul; I shall water it with the gift of my new self disclosure. At that moment I shall grant you a deeper, more spiritual impression of the mystery of my being. For some time I will let you live on this new awareness of who I am. It will nourish and strengthen you until the moment comes that I must withdraw again to leave you in darkness. No image or impression, no matter how sublime, discloses me exhaustively. I will make you grow from impression to impression, from withholding to withholding, from return to return.*

*Finally, in this life or later, my Holy Spirit may reveal me as the ineffable Mystery, hiding in the cloud of unknowing, forever revealing, forever concealing.*

In this way, the Lord repeatedly withdraws. "Where I am going you cannot come." During the ascent of the spirit, darkness descends often. I should be concerned if there is never darkness in my mind or when the flame of "looking for him" has been extinguished in my heart. I might then pray:

"Maybe, Lord, I have lost my love and longing. Maybe I am fixated on an image of you that I idolized as if it were the fullness of your mystery. Meanwhile, you are knocking on my door to manifest yourself to me in a whole new way. Unfortunately, I am not there to open it for you, for I am no longer looking for you in faith and fidelity."

In our love for humanity, for all people of good will, for so many anonymous Christians, we may ask ourselves: Can they too grow by looking for him whom they do not know in Jesus?

Recall the prologue of the Gospel of John, his hymn to the Logos.

Through him all things came to be,
not one thing had its being but through him.

(Jn. 1:3)

Every person, tree, wave of the sea, star, flower, blade of grass, butterfly and molecule have begun in and through the Eternal Word. Before the splendor of the Incarnate Word, there was already the splendor of the creative word animating the dance of stars and planets in the universe, suffusing cosmos, earth and sky. Many men and women of good will are looking for the luminous trails of his passing in the mirror of nature. Looking for the radiant reflection of the Eternal, they fall into the quiet and wonder of contemplation. Although they are not enlightened by the Revelation, Jesus may still grant them the grace of an awareness of the marvels of creation in which divinity shines forth silently. Unknowingly, they too look for him in wonder and expectation.

# IV

# THE MIRACLE OF THE NEW COMMANDMENT

"I give you a new commandment:
love one another;
just as I have loved you,
you must also love one another.
By this love you have for one another,
everyone will know that you are my disciples."

(Jn. 13:34-35)

Jesus will no longer be with his disciples in a visible way, though they will still be with each other. He wants them to love one another just as he loved them while he was still among them. He calls this his new commandment. He does not mean a legal commandment in the tradition of Moses. It is more like a strong, personal appeal, a solemn invitation. It is not new, in the sense that it never existed before. Jesus explains what is new in it by adding that they should love one another "just as I have loved you."

The disciples have experienced what this new love of Jesus means. They are now asked to show that love to one another. Of course, their love, like Jesus', should extend itself to all people. Still here he speaks, first of all, about their love for one another.

People who are gifted by Jesus with the same faith, hope and love can manifest a mutual love and understanding that is not possible in the same way among those who do not share this graced experience. "By this love you have for one another, everyone will know that you are my disciples." This mutual concern and understanding among believers is bound to show itself. People will realize its presence. They may even be drawn into it.

Minucius Felix characterized the Christians as people who "love each other even without knowing each other." Jerome wrote a commentary on the Letters of John. He tells us that John was asked by his Christians why he kept repeating? "Children, love one another." His answer was "because this is the commandment of the Lord, and if we only follow this it is enough."

A mystery of love unites all those who are born of God by grace. This love is not the love of an elite excluding others. The love of Jesus widens the heart; it opens us to all of humanity. Where there is no love, there can be no true Christian life. It is a love based on faith and cannot have any other foundation. This Christian love will not be perfect here on earth; it will reach its fullness only in the Eschaton.

"Lord, you give me a new commandment. Truly it is an unexpected gift. Most human commandments are impositions. Often they seem forbidding. They dry up life and love. They do not lift up mind and heart;

they do not create warmth and intimacy. Your new commandment is a gift, a source of togetherness and healing, the beginning of a community of believers in which respect is primary.

"You tell me to love others just as you have loved me. You not only tell me; you grant me the power to do so. That is what the gift is all about.

"We long for you, but you are no longer with us in the flesh. No longer do you walk the earth. The splendor of your divinity we know in faith. Yet the light of faith is dim to the human mind. But now you promise to be with us in a new way—the way of the gift of your love to be instilled in each of us so that we may be for one another a sign of your generosity.

"You say to us: I command you to carry my consolation to one another. I ask you to sustain each other during the waiting for my second coming. To uplift each other with my own inspiration.

"What a mystery! Your power of love has become mine, has truly taken hold of me. The miracle of your love is in me. I may not feel or sense it, but I know in faith it is truly there, for you have told me so."

We may dislike the other because he is unlike us, yet we can still love others in the Lord and the Lord in them. We must love one another just as he has loved us.

He has loved us as uniquely chosen by the Father from all eternity.

He has loved us as created by him in this space and time.

He has loved us as called forth by the Spirit to a

unique mission in life.

He has loved us to the end; he gave his life for us.

He has loved us before we loved him. He embraced us in spite of our sinfulness, our reluctance, our resistance. His love for us is an ineffable manifestation of what his Father is: He is love.

"Lord, I cannot get over my astonishment, my joy about the love you are. I can sing and dance with Francis of Assisi and cry out to all the world to hear: God is love, love, love.

"And now that same divine love is truly mine. I have been made a tabernacle, a sanctuary, a generator of divine love in the midst of humanity."

The content of our Lord's commandment to love one another is not new. He revealed that to the chosen people long before he became one of us in the flesh. New is the way in which he asks us to love: just as he has loved us. It is the same love the chosen people were invited to show to their neighbors. But our understanding of his love should be deepened immensely. They did not know what we know now. They had not seen the revelation of God's love in Jesus, its manifestation in the manger of Bethlehem, in Nazareth, in his suffering and death on the cross. They did not know that the Son of God would live on in all of us in a whole new way.

"Lord, I can never thank you enough for having chosen me to live in the fullness of time, to have been endowed with this revelation of divine love. Countless holy men and women have waited in vain for this hour of the highest manifestation of God's love. Why have I been destined from eternity to know the fullness of your revelation, the mystery of your incarnation? Who can ponder the depth of your counsel, the secret of your election? I can only kneel down before you and express gratefulness."

The love of Jesus for us is the source of true community of those who believe in him. His love is his presence in and among us. Though we cannot yet see him as our glorified Lord in the splendor of the Trinity, we can see him in the manifestation of his love in us and our fellow believers. We are called to make him present also to others growing in his love and extending it to all people.

"By this love you have for one another, everyone will know that you are my disciples." As a community of believers, we will only be effective when we continue his presence in the world. The only way to make him present is by manifesting his divine love. When people experience how we love one another, Jesus becomes real for them.

"Lord, I see how people need that witness. Everywhere we are faced with their gravest problem, that of communion, of communication, of love for one another. So many are stricken with the terror of isolation. They feel lost and forlorn in a loveless world. How eagerly they seek a remedy. New techniques of encounter are invented almost daily. All of them tend to do some good, to facilitate our readiness for the gift of your divine presence yet I see now that they are in vain if they are not leading us to the deeper ground of our oneness that is you alone."

To be an effective Church is to witness for respectful love of one another in God. No wonder that the early Church placed this commandment among the words it wanted to remember as the last loving words of Jesus. We should return to these words often, ponder them, ask ourselves what they mean for us as a community in Christ. Let us remember how fervently Christ prayed for this oneness:

"May they all be one,
Father, may they be one in us,
as you are in me and I am in you,
so that the world may believe it was you who sent me.
I have given them the glory you gave to me,
that they may be one as we are one.
With me in them and you in me,
may they be so completely one
that the world will realize that it was you who sent me
and that I have loved them as much as you loved me.
                                        (Jn. 17:21-23)

The Incarnate Word adopted us; he filled us with the glory of the Most High. St. Athanasius was inspired to use a marvellous word to express that wonder. He says that we became "verbified!" He means to say that we were taken up in the Divine Word, made over in him. Each of us is "verbified," that is, we participate in his divine love and glory.

"Deepen my faith in this wonder, Jesus. I see so many unpleasant things in myself and others. We are all far from glorious. We are all fraught with pettiness. How is it possible, Lord, to believe in your glory in myself and others in the face of so much ugliness? And what am I to think of the wrongs I see in the history of your Church? How can I believe in your glory in the community of believers I have been called to belong to?"

Such questions may come up in our meditations on Jesus' words. They are not easy to answer, but it may be of some help if we think about Jesus as the Christ of the Transfiguration and as the kenotic Christ . . . Christ on Mt. Tabor, transfigured before the eyes of his disciples and the kenotic Christ St. Paul speaks about.

Kenosis means that Christ emptied himself of visible glory. His glory became the hidden glory of an infant in Bethlehem, the child of simple parents in Nazareth, who later spent most of his life as a laborer. He became the humiliated Christ of the Passion, the Christ on the cross, suffering, forlorn, feeling lost and crying out:

"My God, my God, why have you deserted me?" (Mt. 26:47)

In the transfigured Christ of Mt. Tabor, we see the manifestation of Jesus' visible glory already here on earth. In the Christ of Calvary, we are faced with the mystery of his hidden glory, a humiliated glory seen only by faith. Jesus lived mostly the self-emptying life. Even his disciples could rarely experience the glory of his divinity. When he was transfigured before them, they cried out that they would like to stay there with

him, in the beauty of his glory. But he took them down
from the mountain and told them not to speak about
what they saw to the people. He wanted to continue
the hidden life.

It is the same for us. Jesus' glory is hidden deeply in
our broken lives. Sometimes there is a moment of
transfiguration, a moment of generosity, of loving
presence to others—a moment when we experience the
goodness and kindness of other people—the glory of
God in them. Such a moment of transfiguration
makes us and other poor humans different, more
beautiful, clothed with his glory, a pointer to the glory
that is awaiting us in the Eschaton.

"The hidden glory of you, my kenotic Lord, is also
present in each of us. Help me to love your hidden
glory in the weak ones, in those who are
temperamental, in the sick, the suffering and the
poor, in anxious and tense people, in my own
confused and suffering life. Let me inwardly bow
down in veneration for you, Christ, humiliated and
hidden in each suffering fellow man, in those who
seem fools and failures, in those who cross me, who
hold different values, who threaten me by alien
attitudes.

"Free me from false ideals; let me not build
community on the wrong foundation or on the vain
expectation that anyone or any group can sustain
perfect harmony indefinitely. We are all limited; no
techniques of encounter can transcend our
boundaries. Only you can, my Lord. When we empty
ourselves like you did, kenotic Christ, you may allow

us times of coming together; they will inevitably be followed by discord, by the loss of our wholeness, our at-homeness with one another in your presence.

"The deepest possibility for oneness in community is to realize the glory that you have given to each of us in a way we cannot see, that taxes our trust, that forces us to look at one another in faith alone."

# V

## THE TRUE FOLLOWER OF JESUS

Simon Peter said, "Lord, where are you going?" Jesus replied, "Where I am going you cannot follow me now; you will follow me later." Peter said to him, "Why can't I follow you now? I will lay down my life for you." "Lay down your life for me?" answered Jesus. "I tell you most solemnly, before the cock crows you will have disowned me three times."

(Jn. 13:36-38)

Simon Peter says, "Lord, where are you going?" Peter had heard Jesus' new commandment: to love one another just as he had loved them, but he is not ready to give up Jesus' own company and to be satisfied with that of the disciples. He is not asking where the Lord is going merely out of curiosity or concern. Peter's words express a determination to stay with Jesus in spite of his words of farewell. He does not understand what Jesus means by his departure. Peter loves his master and now that he has to go to his Father, Peter wants to come along. He wants to know more about the destiny the Lord is speaking of.

Jesus replies, "Where I am going you cannot follow me now; you will follow me later." No explanation would have made much sense to the disciples at this moment. He gives a deeper reason why Peter cannot come with him to the Father. The divine direction of Peter's life entails that he will first have to serve the Lord as an apostle. Only then will Providence allow him to follow Jesus: he will die as his master by crucifixion and follow him then to the Father.

Peter says to him: "Why can't I follow you now? I will lay down my life for you."

Peter should have accepted the answer of Jesus. But his impetuousness and willfulness are too strong to give up his determination. He is not really listening to what Jesus says to him. He has little insight into his own weakness; he feels nothing can prevent him from following Jesus even if he would have to lay down his life for him.

"Lay down your life for me?" answers Jesus. "I tell you most solemnly, before the cock crows you will have disowned me three times."

Jesus is forthright. He wants Peter to realize that he lives in illusions about his own strength and courage. He reveals to him that he will try to save his own life by disavowing Jesus loudly, three times, as though he had not even known him. To remind him later of this prediction, the Lord indicates the time that it will happen: this night before the dawn. When the cock crows, Peter will remember the words of Jesus. The Lord, taken past him, will look at him. (Lk. 22:61) Tears of repentance will fill Peter's eyes.

"Lord, Peter's weakness reminds me of my own betrayal. In your presence I often feel enraptured, but my enthusiasm, like Peter's, seems all too human— more excitement of sentiment than of spirit, more a mood than a lasting disposition, more the fruit of imagination than of grace. My fervency is mixed with self reliance.

"I whisper smugly: No matter what happens, Lord, you can count on me. I will follow you everywhere in this world. Don't tell me that I am not ready to go all the way. Nothing shall hold me back, no danger, no threat, no sacrifice. My life counts for nothing. For your sake I will lay it down gladly every day. You can build on me. I will always own up to your love.

"When I quiet down inwardly, when I silence excitement and still the noise of sentiment, the roar of enthusiasm, I recall my weakness. Without you I can do nothing."

Jesus is the Risen Lord at the heart of our humanity. He dwells in the midst of human history. Emerging daily in his risen presence through human generations, he slowly breaks this history open to a new and wondrous light. People resist him and fight this new creation, but through those who follow him, he keeps emerging persistently. His disciples are a gentle force of transfiguration of this earth. They have not chosen him; he has chosen them. It is he who calls them to join the procession through centuries and generations of those who radiate light into the darkness of human life.

"Only you, Jesus, do the timing; only you assign

each of us his limited place in this drama of salvation. It is you alone who endow us with the grace and power to follow you in the way you want us to at every moment of our lives. I cannot invite myself to your service. Let me never pretend that I can choose my own place among those who follow you."

In the beginning of the spiritual life, it may be sentiment that rules our day. We think it is the Lord speaking, but it is only our imagination. We love our own excitement and think we love him alone.

To pierce our illusion, to deflate our arrogance, he may allow us to fail many times. Some of our best resolves may come to nought.

He may even allow us to forget him. We begin to live out of a worldly spirit, a secret self centeredness. We don't heed his inspirations; we disown him in the midst of our day. Our life seems to say: "I don't know the man"—the same words Peter used that fateful night.

We live in forgetfulness. We start the morning by offering our day to him. Within an hour we are swept up in bustling activity with no thought of his presence. We lose our connecting thread to the Divine. We will dwell in darkness until a ray of his presence touches us. That ray is a signal of his grace telling us gently: *You have forgotten me, but I have not forgotten you. I love you so much that I could never forget you.*

That ray may be some sudden event, some word of a friend, some gesture of a simple soul, some suffering or pain or failure. We must never silence these signals. They mean that he is calling us back to our deepest self, that a new grace is awaiting us, the grace of sorrow and repentence, of humility and insight into our nothingness. True spiritual life is a life of walking in the truth of who we are.

"It is not I, Lord, who own you, but you who own me. The only thing I can do by myself is to disown you. It is arrogance to think that I can follow you anywhere, any way, any time on my own initiative.

"Now I understand a little better, my Lord, your coming and going. Often I feel left alone in the everydayness of a life that seems empty without you: a dull life of merely doing things, of bearing with others resentfully. Deepen my trust in what you told Peter and what you tell me, that we will follow you later.

"I realize the tremendous emotional love Peter had for you. I see now that this fervor at the beginning of the spiritual life is by no means the deepest, most stable and solid kind of love. Purify my feelings; let me walk in the dryness of the desert in faithfulness to you. Then my love may become deep and true. Thank you for cutting through my rapture and enthusiasm. When you go away, when your light disappears from my life, I feel paralyzed, unable to do the things I said I would do in my excited imagination. I should never feel too sure about consolation. My faith will grow mainly when I long for your presence and discover it in your absence."

We live not only the life of the Spirit but also a life of resistance to the Spirit. A life of secret pride and ambition, of oversensitivity and excessive concern. A small life questioned by the signals of his grace: at the moment of illness or pain, of losing a dear one, of slander and misunderstanding, of seeing that community, friends or family are not as marvelous as we dreamt them to be. These moments of truth are meant to make us question our life. Was it rooted in faith? Or was it rooted in human suppositions: environments we believed unchangeable, a future we had all figured out, success and popularity that came easily our way?

"At the moment of truth, enable me to lay down my life for you. That life of false expectations, of vain dreams about the perfect friend, family, church or community. Thank you for questioning over and over again that idle life by touching it with suffering and pain, with disappointment and dismal failure, so that I may lay it down and follow you."

Often we don't listen to his signs. We don't lay down our life for Jesus. We disown the Lord. Our daily deeds belie that we know him; the cock keeps crowing in vain. Instead of owning our life in Jesus, we cling to a life of our own. He is calling forth our true self in the midst of disappointment and we disown his call.

He wants us to try peacefully to improve ourselves, our family, our community, the world in which we live, and the history in which we participate. What he does not want is a loss of peace and trust when our best attempts fail miserably. To be overly upset, to be in despair, to be filled with resentment is to disown his holy presence in human history, to prefer spectacular change to the silent mystery of slow and unseen transformation.

Even if we disown the Lord three times and more, as we know from the story of Peter, we should not despair. We should ask humbly for the grace to be his own again, to become faithful to his hidden glory in this world. Peter grew slowly over a lifetime in loyalty to Jesus. He began to lay down his life for him day by day. The final laying down of his life in death was the crowning of the daily discipleship that wove his existence into a beautiful tribute of love and loyalty to his Lord alone.

## VI

## TRUST AND TRANSFORMATION

"Do not let your hearts be troubled.
Trust in God still, and trust in me."

(Jn. 14:1)

The disciples felt badly. They had just heard Jesus
say that even Peter would deny him. They admired
Peter as a brave, outspoken man, a loyal leader. If
even he would fail, what about them?

They felt badly. The master had told them that he
would leave them, that they would try in vain to find
him, that one of them would betray him. All these
words hinted at something terrible in store for Jesus,
for all of them. Foreboding and fright filled their
hearts. To hear Jesus say such things was agony for
those men who loved him and believed in his success
in Israel. To relieve their anguish, to encourage and
console, he begins to reassure them.

He tells them that their hearts should not be
troubled, that things will be all right in the long run,
that they should trust in him.

In Chapter Fourteen many reasons are given why

they should not lose heart. The most important of
them is the promise of a great, new presence in our
midst: the presence of the Spirit, the consoler, the
steady helper, the gentle advocate.

Jesus gives three main reasons for courage and trust
during our pilgrimage. He tells us first of all that he
will not always stay away from us (1-12a). He promises
to send us the Holy Spirit as a consoler and helper
(12b-17). He assures us also that he himself will
remain in our midst but in a whole new way (18-24).
Then, towards the end of this Chapter, we hear him
taking up again these promises but now in the
opposite order. We are told that the Father and the
Son will come and live in us (20-24); that the Paraclete
will help us to penetrate deeper into his teachings (25-
26); that he himself will go to the Father where he will
be better able to help us (27-31).

This message of consolation begins with the words:
"Do not let your hearts be troubled. Trust in God still,
and trust in me."

John uses the words believing, trusting, having
faith, in a special way. He speaks about trusting *in*,
believing *in*, having faith *in*. Faith in this sense does
not mean simply that I say "yes" only in my mind to
statements made by Jesus or by his Church. It goes
deeper; it is an attitude that embraces all I am, think
and feel. The word "belief" in the Hebrew scriptures
goes back to a simple Semitic word, familiar to all of
us: *Amen*—a call to belief, often used by Jesus when
he makes an important statement in John's Gospel.

*Amen* can mean truly, in truth, indeed, really, "so

it is for sure." We use the word *Amen,* therefore, at the end of our creed and our prayers. We express and affirm briefly our faith in what we have stated. We say that we stand behind it, believe in it with our whole being. Or, when another has said the prayer, we answer *Amen* to manifest emphatically that we approve of it, identify with it, surrender to it and through it to the God to whom we pray.

Originally *Amen* meant: reliable, trustworthy, dependable. The corresponding verb *aman* meant: to lean on God as upon a rock, to put our security in him. How often he is called a rock in the psalms we sing. In this way the people of Israel were reminded constantly that God alone was the firm ground on which Israel stood, that they should find strength and security in Yahweh only.

Over the centuries that trust in God as their rock has been exemplified in the history of the Jewish people in the diaspora. Persecuted, ridiculed, closed off in their ghettoes, discriminated against, burnt at the stake, they put their trust in Yahweh alone. It is the faith that says: even if I have to travel through a dark valley, I do not fear danger or disaster, for you are with me.

This trust of the Jewish believers touches us more today when many of us are exposed to a diaspora experience of our own. Jesus tells his disciples in this hour of farewell to maintain this trust of all Jewish believers:

*As good Jewish men, put all your trust in God alone. He is your stronghold and your rock. You share*

*in that trust in the Divine that is the greatest gift of the
best of your people. Don't give that up. Trust still in
God, as you learned so well as sons of Israel. But I add
something to it: trust also in me. Trust in me just as
you trust in the God of Israel. Let me too be your rock,
your stronghold.*

We can only have faith in a person who, as a firm
ground, carries everything. Only on such a rock can
we lean safely, no matter what happens. No human
being can be that rock. For man is like grass that
thrives today and tomorrow fades away. When Jesus
asks his disciples to trust him as they trusted God
himself, he tells them that he too is that rock, that he
is one with his Father whom they and their people had
trusted for so long.

Not only the hearts of the apostles but also our
hearts are often troubled. Their painful situation
symbolizes our situation until the Lord returns in
glory.

Often we feel discouraged by the demonic power
which opposes the defenseless power of divine love in
this world. Our hearts are troubled when the Lord
hides his face and his glory, when the feats of unbelief
seem splendid and triumphant and those of faith
pitiful and feeble.

This recurrent situation of his disciples in the world
is symbolized by the apostles at this moment. Losing
his bodily presence, they lose their anchor, their grip,
their only support. These simple men had clung to
him more than they realized. Their very life was linked
with his. It had become meaningful in his light. His

success, they believed, would be theirs. But he tells them he will go away, leaving them alone. Only one thing can offset this loss, this loneliness, only one consolation is possible in this desolation, only one light can shine in this darkness: faith in Jesus.

Faith is more than something we have; it is what we are through his grace alone; it is putting our ultimate certainty not in ourselves but in him, no matter what happens. When he gives us this basic trust in him, he grants us an awareness that he embodies the Mystery of the Divine, of the Father. He asks us to say "yes" to him and through him to the Father. Trust in God still and trust in me.

This loving trust he asks of us is much more than a yes to a statement or creed. To trust in him is to meet him, to come to know him, to make our home in him. To trust in him means also to allow him to make his home in us, to fill us with eternity, to transport us from death to life. The moment we trust in him, we are raised out of darkness into his light. Even though we die, we will live because we are raised up to lasting life in Jesus. Our trust will not be in vain. His presence in us will transform our life.

Trusting in him, we will discover our unique graced self, hidden in God; we will be born anew from him. We become God's child. Therefore, we are called to host the Paraclete, to envision the splendor of the Lord, and to do the works for humanity that Jesus himself did, yes, even greater works. With other men and women, full of faith, we will form a community of love in the midst of humanity, the community of those whom John calls "sons of light." (Jn. 12:36)

"Trusting in you, my Lord, is finding my firmness and safety, the ultimate direction and meaning of my life outside of my own limitations. It is the leap of faith beyond the borders of the here and now. I trust that my life today and tomorrow will be meaningful because of you. With my fellow believers, I trust that you will return to fulfill the divine mystery of human culture and history.

"In this holy trust we build the earth. With you we empty ourselves out in service of a redeemed world in the labor pains of transformation. With you we are the grain of wheat which, by dying in holy kenosis, fosters life in unfolding humanity.

"Trust in you enables us to embrace human history wholeheartedly, not to escape it in isolated piety which finds no incarnation in daily surroundings.

"To disdain the attempt to transform this earth is a subtle form of despair. To seek you, Lord, apart from our history is to lack trust in you."

# VII

## AT HOME IN FATHER'S HOUSE

"There are many rooms in my Father's house; if there were not, I should have told you."

(Jn. 14:2-3)

Jesus had spoken of leaving the apostles. He had asked them to love each other when he would no longer be with them. He had predicted to Peter, who insisted on going with him, that he would disown Jesus. All of this was understandably discouraging for these simple men who could not grasp what Jesus was talking about.

The Master tries to comfort them by explaining the good that would result from his departure. Already at the beginning of Chapter Fourteen, we read his admonishment: "Do not let your hearts be troubled. Trust in God still, and trust in me." He wanted to convince them that there was no reason for them to be so shaken at the thought of his going away.

His departure, when seen in its deepest meaning and consequences, should not be a cause of distress but an occasion of joy mingled with sadness. They should trust in God and in Jesus in all things, also this departure. For the departure means that Jesus is completing the mission of his Father; that he, in returning to the Father, will open the inner, eternal life of God for them and for all who will follow Jesus in faith and fidelity.

Though the events of the coming days will be disturbing to the disciples, they must keep on trusting God and Jesus. The ground for his demand that they should have the same trust in him as in God is his divinity. (Jn. 10:30; 14:9; Mt. 16:16)

Trying to comfort them, Jesus goes on: "There are many rooms in my Father's house; if there were not, I should have told you." The Greek word used here for rooms or mansions means lasting dwelling places. The scriptures use such expressions, first of all, to point to heaven. We cannot conceive what life with God will be like in the hereafter. Therefore, the writers of the scriptures prefer figurative language to exact descriptions to point to what God's dwelling place is.

Jesus calls this dwelling place "my Father's house." This phrasing deepens our awareness that God is really a Father to us. He is presented as having a home to which we are all invited. The warmth and tenderness the word "home" evokes in us is in this metaphor; it makes us humanly aware of the infinite love awaiting us at the end of our mission in this world.

This interpretation does not mean, however, that the house of the Father would have no meaning for us in our everyday life on earth. St. Paul assures us:

"You are no longer aliens or foreign visitors; you are citizens like all the saints, and part of God's household." (Ep. 2:19) We belong already here to the household of the Father; we are already living in Father's house.

St. Paul suggests that to be in the house of the Father is to be in Jesus: "You are part of a building that has the apostles and prophets for its foundations, and Christ Jesus himself for its main cornerstone. As every structure is aligned on him, all grow into one holy temple in the Lord; and you too, in him, are being built into a house where God lives, in the Spirit. (Ep. 2:20-22)

The statement about the *"many"* mansions should not be misunderstood to mean that all kinds of people with all sorts of convictions and comportments will indiscriminately find a place in the house of the Father. They will only if they are people of good will who honestly try to live up to their graced convictions in spite of repeated failings.

Once people are true believers who share the same fundamental spirituality taught by Jesus, they may vary much in their special or personal spiritualities. The latter particularize the spirituality of Jesus in tune with one's culture, temperament, life call, and personal history. In that sense, all of these true followers of Jesus can find a room among the many in the house of the Father.

As St. Paul again asserts: ". . . you are, all of you, sons of God through faith in Christ Jesus. All baptized in Christ, you have all clothed yourselves in Christ,

and there are no more distinctions between Jew and
Greek, slave and free, male and female, but all of you
are one in Christ Jesus." (Ga. 3:26-28)

All true Christians, no matter how different in
cultural background, social status, male or female
characteristics, will thus find a room among the many
rooms in Father's house.

"If there were not, I should have told you." The
notion of the many rooms is not something new to the
disciples. The entire Old Testament had always said
so. Jesus himself had indicated often that his love had
prepared salvation for many. Jesus assures the
disciples that it is really so; otherwise he would have
told them. He says this to ready them for the promise
that his departure will make it possible for him to
prepare places for them in the house of the Father.
They should thus feel comforted and be glad.

"Your words about the many rooms touch me,
Lord. With St. Paul I love to think about you yourself
as 'Father's house.' A house that I am called to live in.
You invite me to make that house my home. The
house you are is available to all, but few make it their
home, their dwelling place. Few try to live in and with
you."

The house of creation was the first dwelling place
given to humanity—a house that came to be in and
through the Creative Word, a house upheld by his
enduring creative presence. This house is to be made a
home by mankind; it is to be transformed gradually by
each one of us.

How we have failed our task as homemakers! We

betrayed our calling. We refused to share the transformation of world and universe. We were more concerned with our own gain than with the unfolding of creation. We tried to amass money and power at the expense of a graced expansion of humanity and nature. We preferred our own ease to the ease of our brothers and sisters in a beautified house of creation where love and justice would reign supreme.

Left on our own, we sabotaged the will of the Father. We turned creation into a den of iniquity. We spoiled nature; we depleted its treasures so that only few could live complacent lives in cold and loveless splendor. What was meant to be a home for all has been turned into a hell for many.

"Creative Word, thank you for not leaving us orphans, battling each other while destroying creation. You became one of us. You lived before our eyes a life that shows how even the most simple person in an unknown town or neighborhood can share in the homemaking of humanity. You did not leave us alone after your departure. You saw in compassion how we ruined your house, yet you offered yourself to mankind as a new house of the Father."

Once we have made our home in him, we will find the strength that true homes give us. Making him our home shall enable us to venture out from him into the house of creation and to help make it a home again for suffering humanity.

Since the resurrection, Jesus permeates cosmos and world with a new mode of presence. In each human heart he whispers his invitation to share in the glory of his resurrection. Let us enjoy and admire the glorious house of the Father that is the Risen Lord. Let us make our home in him.

People who refuse to do so will suffer loneliness and isolation. He is the source of oneness and cooperation: he, the Christ, the house of the Father.

If we truly make our home in him, he will make his home in us. We will become one with others who choose him too as their source of life. He has prayed that we may find this unity:

"May they all be one,
Father, may they be one in us,
as you are in me and I am in you,
so that the world may believe it was you who sent me.
I have given them the glory you gave to me,
that they may be one as we are one.
With me in them and you in me,
may they be so completely one
that the world will realize that it was you who sent me
and that I have loved them as much as you loved me."

(Jn. 17:21-23)

When we make our home in him, many more may hear the call to make the house of creation a gracious home for all people. But first they have to enter into the new divine dwelling place that is Jesus.

The baptism of water or desire was our entrance into that residence. The Incarnate Word opened for us the door of his dwelling. We were taken up in the Word, made over in him. Each of us shares in his glory.

The art of living in Jesus has been lost by many. We have become less sensitive to the gentle presence of the Holy One in our midst. Fascinated by the lights of this earth, we have become blind to the light that is Jesus. His glory among us is as hidden as that of the infant in the cradle of Bethlehem, a poor child of poor parents, a fugitive in Egypt, a laborer in Nazareth, an unlettered, itinerant preacher, a defeated man on a cross, feeling lost and crying out:

"My God, my God, why have you deserted me?"
(Mt. 27:46)

"Thank you, Lord, for the many rooms in Father's house. No matter my peculiarities, sinfulness and imperfections, there is room for me. You want me to respect the life space of each Christian in your dwelling place. Some are born with a pleasant disposition, but most must cope with poor endowment, with wounds inflicted by well-meaning parents and teachers, with anxiety, envy and sensuality. In spite of my efforts, I too fall back into habits that obscure your grace, that hide the glory of your presence. Yet one of the rooms in your house remains destined for me from eternity.

"Help me to love your presence in my failing self, in the weak, the temperamental, the sick, the anxious, the tense who dwell in your house."

Respect for all who dwell in him is a way to true community. No matter how we love him, any community of Christmas on earth will be one of sinners where his glory will be hidden.

His grace creates in his house not a community of the perfect but one of mercy and of faith. To build community outside him is to build on a faulty foundation. Let us not nourish false expectations about community living. We will be caught in disappointments. We are often a disillusion for one another. We should not be disheartened by daily failure. We must believe in the hiddenness of his glory in one another, no matter how disappointed we are.

Psychological insights are helpful, but they are peripheral means to true community. The deepest possibility for oneness in diversity is to look at one another in the graced conviction that there are many rooms in Father's house for many kinds of fellow believers. The same is true of the Church, the visible manifestation of the house of the Father.

"Teach me, Lord, to bear with limitation not only in myself and in others, but also in your Church on earth.

"Your Church, Lord, is the image of the house of the Father. Your Church shares the hiddenness of your glory; it is a Church not of saints but of sinners, a Church wounded by the vagaries of history. Each time this image of your house declines in outer glory, there should be an increase in my faith.

"Your Church makes its way through the maze of history; it unfolds while groping with new manifestations of human culture. Your Church finds its way laboriously over the millenia. I revere you, hidden Lord, in your suffering Church, in the stumbling Christians of this first hour of Christianity. We are the awkward pioneers of the early millenia of your little flock. Many millenia hence people may smile about the mistakes we made. But you allowed the infancy of your Church to unfold through our confused minds and hearts. We often fail, yet we love you in our failing selves. Grant us the strength to renew our mission of mutual love, to affirm one another as members of your household so that the world will realize that

'. . . it was you who sent me
and that I have loved them as much as you loved me.' "

(Jn. 17:23)

## VIII

## GOING TO THE PLACE
## GOD HAS PREPARED

"I am going now to prepare a place for you,
and after I have gone and prepared you a place,
I shall return to take you with me;
so that where I am
you may be too.
You know the way to the place where I am going."

(Jn. 14:2-4)

Jesus has assured us that there are many rooms in his Father's house. This assurance means that many kinds of people and life styles may find a home in him. He is the visible appearance of the Divine for all of us. He is really Emmanuel, God with us.

Perhaps his assurance that there is room in his house for every true Christian was evoked by the excitement of Peter when he told Jesus that he would never betray him, that he would lay down his life for him.

Peter showed the weakness of his temperament. He was a volatile man, still too much of an anxious person, fearful of soldiers and dignitaries. Not knowing his limits, he had little self insight, made grandiose promises, but betrayed them when anxiety took over. It is as if Jesus told him not to trust in himself but only in God, to trust in God in spite of his betrayal and the lack of balance in his impetuous personality. It was as if he tried to tell Peter that he could wholeheartedly trust him when he said that there is room in his Father's house even for such a boisterous and unstable Christian as Peter is.

By his death Jesus was able to prepare a unique place for us, a lasting place in eternity. This unique preparation begins here on earth from the day of our conception to the moment of our transition to eternal life. It is his Spirit in us who prepares us daily by helping us to find our unique self direction in and with him. He speaks in us and in our life situation.

The Spirit makes us aware of ourselves as a work of the Creative Word. He reveals to us our limits and possibilities within our genetic and spiritual endowment; these point to the self direction meant for us by our Creator.

He gives us insights also into workings of grace beyond our created nature. Briefly, he discloses to us over a lifetime God's manifestations in us as Creative Word and as Incarnate Word. These manifestations do not oppose but sustain each other; they point in unison to one and the same self direction.

In and through this emergent self direction, Jesus prepares a place for us here on earth and in eternity. If we try to be faithful to this preparation—even if we do not succeed—he shall return and take us with him, so that where he is, we may be too. If our life in the end has not yet reached the fullness for which he tried to prepare it, he will purify and complement this lack before taking us totally with him where he is.

His Spirit, who prepares us daily, could only come to live in us after Jesus had given his life for us. St. Irenaeus, the Church Father, says that his Holy Spirit had first to become accustomed to living in one nature; namely, in Jesus'. Only then would he come to live in all of his followers. So before the Spirit came to live in each of us, he was living only in our Lord. It is through the Spirit that we pray:

"Risen Savior, I received your Spirit. Now I am able in his light to find out gradually what my unique room is in you. You are the vine, Jesus, and I am one of your countless branches. As a unique branch, I am prepared by you and your Spirit to bring forth a kind of grape that will nourish humanity in a unique way—provided I accept your preparation of my place in Father's house.

"I may refuse because I want to be somebody I am not. I may live under the tyranny of a self image that is at odds with the place you meant for me. I may dislike the slow and gradual pace of self discovery your Spirit allows me. I want to reach quickly the place destined for me. But you allow me only to disclose my destiny slowly over a lifetime of trial and error.

"I long to be at once perfectly patient, totally gentle, masterfully efficient. You know better than I that such a sudden transformation would make me full of myself, would diminish the experience of my need for you. Therefore, only slowly does your Spirit disclose to me the height and depth of the mystery of the place you are preparing for me. This preparation of my place is a lifelong endeavor.

"I delay this work of your Spirit by my propensity for self deception. Many and devious are the paths of illusion which lead me away from my true place in your Father's house.

"To find my place, I must be open to all sides of myself. I must not consider only what seems praiseworthy in my life; neither should I attend only to my faults and limitations. I should live in relaxed acceptance of what you allow me to be now *at this moment*. Faith helps me to see all my experiences as opportunities to be prepared by you for my place."

We, too, like Peter, can look back on many moments of betrayal. We betrayed Jesus then and we have betrayed him again and again. Why not admit it to ourselves and to him? Why not accept ourselves, as Peter did? Acknowledgment of our weakness enables us to accept what we are at this moment. To make this weakness a stepping stone towards our place in Father's house comes later; accepting the weakness as ours comes first.

The Spirit urges us to be sincere in our openness to his disclosures. He grants us the grace to see what he discloses: the longings, ambitions and aspirations that take us away from the place he wants for us.

As we grow in understanding of our divine self direction, it becomes easier for us to accept our place in life—not the place we ourselves want to carve out or which others want to impose on us, but the place Jesus is preparing for us. We may experience a joyful, liberating moment when we accept our place in his kingdom and the pace of its preparation as ordained by him.

"Spirit of my Lord, you sometimes speak to me through others. You make them your collaborators in the work of my preparation. You may use a true friend or spouse, a counselor or spiritual director who knows me well and cares for me. He tells me what fosters and hinders my true self direction and still accepts me totally as I am, here and now. Thank you Lord, for the gifts of such fellow Christians who are willing to accompany me on my pilgrimage to a mysterious place still hidden for me and known to you alone."

My poor self is thus infinitely loved by Jesus. He has gone to prepare a place for me. He shall return to take that confused self of mine with him; so that where he is, I may be too. Listening to his Spirit means receiving from him, moment by moment, the mystery of my unique place in his Kingdom.

I experience myself, like Peter and the other apostles, as fallible and frail, ready to betray him and the direction he gives to my life, yet capable, with his grace, of finding my place. Then, when he returns to take me with him, I shall be at once what he wanted me to be. In him, I shall shine forth as the lasting unique self he intended me to be from the beginning of time.

## IX

## JESUS, THE WAY TO THE FATHER

"You know the way to the place where I am going."
Thomas said, "Lord, we do not know where you are going,
so how can we know the way?" Jesus said: "I am the Way,
the Truth and the Life. No one can come to the Father
except through me." (Jn. 14:4-7)

Jesus has just told his disciples where he is going
and that his departure means that he will be preparing
a place for them. He now adds another assurance:
"You know the way to the place where I am going."
He does not mean the way he himself will have to take
in the coming days. He speaks about the way the
disciples have to go to reach the place he has promised
them. It is a way they already know, a road they are
already travelling. He has been teaching them that
way since they joined him. They have only to continue
on this path to keep growing in Jesus until he returns
to take them with him forever to the house of the
Father.

"Thomas said, 'Lord, we do not know where you

are going, so how can we know the way?' " Thomas takes for granted that all the disciples feel the way he does. He speaks for all of them when he disagrees with Jesus. They do not even know his destination so how can he think that they know the way to such an unknown place? It is not that Thomas does not believe in Jesus. He does, but he is confused. He would like more clarity in this matter. His faith is not yet strong enough to surrender gladly to Jesus' words even in the midst of the darkness of not understanding. Our Lord does not rebuke Thomas. He tries to make things clearer by explaining that he himself is the way he is pointing to.

What Thomas could not imagine was that Jesus' work would continue beyond the boundary of his life on earth. For him the whole mission of Jesus was to establish the messianic kingdom in Israel. (Ac. 1:6) How could that happen if he was to leave for another place? What about their project? He feels more and more downhearted. Finally he cannot keep his feelings to himself and so blurts out somewhat indignantly: "Lord, we do not know where you are going, so how can we know the way?"

The situation is not as bad as Thomas feels it to be. The disciples know more than they realize. Their sadness has blinded them. Jesus reminds them of what they already know when he says: "I am the Way, the Truth and the Life. No one can come to the Father except through me."

They almost certainly knew this from his daily teachings. Jesus reminds them of these teachings so that they may relate them to the words he has spoken so far this evening. He hopes that a new insight may result which will solve Thomas' problem and take away their misgivings. He summarizes in simple words all that he has taught them, the whole meaning of his life.

Jesus tells them that he himself is the way. "The Way" is an image of himself and his function in their spiritual life. He clarifies this image with two other words: "the Truth and the Life," adding that no one can come to the Father except through him. "Way" has thus to be understood as "means". Jesus himself is the only means to come to the Father.

He does not say as wise men and gurus may, that he will *show* the way but, "I *am* the Way." Nor, like certain thinkers, does he claim: I *have* the truth, but "I *am* the Truth." Not merely: I *lead* to life, as a holy preacher or spiritual director sent by God, but "I *am* the Life."

Jesus had earlier described himself as the one and only way when he said: "When I am lifted up from the earth, I shall draw all men to myself." (Jn. 12:32) Isaiah depicts our predicament before we found the one way that is Jesus: "We had all gone astray like sheep, each following his own way." (Is. 53:6) Only the way that is Jesus leads to the Father. This way is not a doctrine, an ideology, a set of spiritual exercises; it is a person, one person: Jesus Christ. All other ways or means to reach God will be in vain if they do not somehow end in the Way.

Each of the three words, Way, Truth, Life, has its

own content. Yet they are interconnected. They clarify each other. Together they tell us who Jesus is and what he should mean in our life. The order of the words is interesting too. The more we walk this way, the more the truth of God's being becomes known to us; and the more this truth lights up for us and makes us share in it, the more we grow in divine life.

That Jesus is the truth does not mean merely that he is a trustworthy person who speaks the truth. It means that Jesus is everything the Father is but made manifest and accessible to humanity. When Jesus says that he is the truth, he tells in fact that he is the very experience of the Father. He makes this clear when he adds: "No one can come to the Father except through me. If you know me, you know my Father too. From this moment you know him and have seen him." (Jn. 6b-7)

To experience Jesus as the Truth is to experience the Father in Jesus. We must assent in faith to this experience of the Truth of God's being. Then, we are "of the truth;" we "walk in the light." As Jesus said about himself as the Truth: "I am the light of the world; anyone who follows me will not be walking in the dark; he will have the light of life." (Jn. 8:12)

In this light of the Truth, we begin truly to live. We are freed from the shackles of our past; the future is opened up for us; our desire for infinite love will be fulfilled. This liberating knowledge of Divine Truth in Jesus will find its consummation in the Eschaton when: "We shall be like him because we shall see him as he really is." (1 Jn. 3:2)

To grow in the living truth of divine life that Jesus is, we have to make his word our home: "If you make my word your home you will indeed be my disciples, you will learn the truth and the truth will make you free." (Jn. 8: 31-23) Without Jesus, our only Mediator, no way, no truth, no life are left.

Jesus tells his friends: "You know the way to the place where I am going." The place where Jesus is going cannot be a limited spot, well circumscribed in space far away from us. The Lord is not taking off for a distant planet. The place he is going to is not really a place but a person. His going is a passing through death to the Father, taking humanity with him in the end. His going is a re-entrance, but now with his glorified human body, into the divinity, a return into

".  .  . that glory I had with you
before even the world was."

(Jn. 14:5)

His going is not a traversing of a spatial distance; it is the integration of his humanity into the Holy Trinity. Since that reimmersion, the power of Jesus' humanity is everywhere present. The place where he is going is every place. Since his resurrection, there is no spot that is not suffused by the power of his presence. He has become our Way, our Truth, our Life.

"Lord, you are our way to God. You take us with you to the Father. By taking on our nature, you changed each of us. You are our new life. You infused us with divine life, the life of the Father."

This last discourse prepares for the hour in which that life of the Father will come forth in glory as God's gift to us. Since that hour, the life and the Spirit will be given to each of us abundantly by Jesus. If we would only be still and listen, we would hear him daily cry out to us:

"Do not be afraid; it is I,
the *First* and the *Last*; I am the Living One,
I was dead and now I am to live for ever and ever . . ."
(Rev. 1:17-18)

"If any man is thirsty, let him come to me!
Let the man come and drink who believes in me!"

As scripture says: From his breast shall flow fountains of living water. (Jn. 7:37-39)

What is the Way, the Truth, the Life Christ claims to be? Can it be expressed in one powerful word? John gives the answer. That word is *love*.

God is love
and anyone who lives in love lives in God,
and God lives in him. (1 Jn. 4:16)

Anyone who fails to love can never have known God,
because God is love. (1 Jn. 4:8)

God's life *is* love. Making Jesus' way ours is sharing his life of love.

My dear people,
let us love one another

since love comes from God
and everyone who loves is begotten by God and knows
God. (1 Jn. 4:7)

"Jesus, you are the manifestation of the life of the
Father, which is love. You cannot be my way, my
truth, my life if I cut myself off from love, if I do not
care for people and their history; for their social and
cultural unfolding within your creation. In you I am
reborn as a child of divine love:

Think of the love that the Father has lavished on us,
by letting us be called God's children;
and that is what we are. (1 Jn. 3:1)

"This rebirth in you lifts me high above my own
ability to care for others. Your power of love is
implanted in the midst of my vulnerable human love.
Mysteriously transformed, my love may radiate your
divine care for humanity and its unfolding. I begin to
love the people you created with the same love with
which you loved me. This love is the sign that you
yourself have become my way, my truth, my life.

"I give you a new commandment:
love one another;
just as I have loved you,
you also must love one another.
By this love you have for one another,
everyone will know that you are my disciples."
(Jn. 13:34-35)

"No religious or mystical experience of your

presence in me remains true and faithful if I do not try
to live effectively your life of love. If I refuse to walk
the path of love, I cannot retain the true experience of
God. Without love, I cannot see you as you are."

My dear people,
this is not a new commandment that I am writing to
   tell you,
but an old commandment
that you were given from the beginning,
the original commandment which was the message
   brought to you.
Yet in another way, what I am writing to you,
and what is being carried out in your lives as it was
   in his,
is a new commandment;
because the night is over
and the real light is already shining.
Anyone who claims to be in the light
but hates his brother
is still in the dark.
But anyone who loves his brother is living in the light
and need not be afraid of stumbling;
unlike the man who hates his brother and is in the
   darkness,
not knowing where he is going,
because it is too dark to see.

                      (1 Jn. 2:7-11)

    All of us are called to traverse the same Way which
is Christ himself. The true spiritual life of each
Christian is a life of love in Christ for the Father and
humanity. The infinite love of Christ is refracted in
the limited love and care each unique Christian is

called to realize in this world.

To be open to the Way, the Truth, the Life, we should find the unique task and expression of divine love Jesus wants in our lives. In countless loving and caring ways, we can put ourselves in our daily tasks and encounters, but only one way can build the style of divine caring each of us is uniquely called to by the Lord.

There are many tempting possibilities to care in ways that are at odds with the way Christ wants to express care in us. We may try to live a style of love we are not called to. We may want to concretize our care for people in a task or movement not attuned to our individual nature. We may do so to please others because we crave to be liked. Or we may want to belong to a popular social or apostolic movement. We join it blindly in spite of the fact that their particular manifestation of Christ's love is not necessarily ours.

"Only when I root myself in your life, Jesus, hidden deep within me can I find the kind of care you want to live out in me. I should follow your inspiration even if others chide me for not walking popular paths. There is no blueprint. My love cannot be a carbon copy of that of any other Christian. I am called to manifest the Way, the Truth, the Life in a special and unrepeatable fashion.

"My personal life call is like a lamp in which your Way, Truth and Life light up for me uniquely. Each Christian carries the light of his own life direction, his own mode of love. Each experiences you as Way, Truth and Life in a slightly different fashion. Your

Way is not a restricting stereotype. Following you means that in my life of love I must be true to myself and to your example.

"You want me also to be careful not to confuse you as *the* Way with any special way of following you practiced by Christians in a certain cultural period, in one country or century, or in one school of spirituality. There are many who have wisely adapted your Way to their passing situation. Their adaptation, while excellent for them, may not be the best one for me. They met you as Way, Truth and Life in a style that made sense to them, but now their view of the way may not appeal to us who live in another society."

Christians today have to embody Christ's love in many life styles and positions. They have to find their own special way of making him present for family, friends, neighbors and colleagues. We should realize that we are not living him as Way, Truth and Life if our existence has deteriorated into a set of cliche postures borrowed blindly from Christians of former cultures and generations. Our life should be guided by our own experience of him. Then our way will be in tune not only with our surroundings but also with the mystery and dynamics of our own interiority which God respects so deeply.

"Let me share in your infinite respect for my unique calling. Awaken me to my way in and with you. Never let me be satisfied with a dull, mediocre life of petty schemes for popularity, power and possessions. Without the inspiration of your Way, I may lose my own. Presence to you as the Way will compel me to examine my everyday existence and its motivations. I will no longer lull myself into mediocrity by taking the easy course. My small way will gain immense power and beauty by its immersion in the Way that is you.

"Without you, my way leads nowhere. Without you, my way does not find its infinite end in the Father. In you I realize how my way finds also its beginning in Him.

"Thank you, Lord, for your message in this discourse. The source of my peace must be my faith and trust in God. Trust in God must be the same as trust in you because you are God. You tell me not to be worried about my peculiarities, my weaknesses, my limits. For you assure me there are many rooms in my Father's house. I don't have to worry about the way to Father's house because you are the Way, the Truth, the Life. My growth in the spiritual life is never the mere result of what I am doing. The Way is already there, given in you. I have only to surrender, to believe in you, to say *yes* to you. At that moment I am healed.

"This trust, surrender and faith in the Way is the deepest source of my spiritual life. It is your gift to me. How mistaken I was in my preoccupation with the works I should be doing to please you and to gain heaven. I should open up first of all to you as the Way, the Truth, and Life. No matter where I go, the house of the Lord is waiting for me. No matter my worry and weakness, I am already at home in you. Only I don't believe it enough; I don't surrender enough. I still think too often that I have to do it all.

"Deepen my faith that there is a room for each of us in your Father's house. Strengthen my trust in you as Way, Truth and Life."

# X

## SEEING THE FATHER IN JESUS

"No one can come to the Father except through me. If you know me, you know my Father too. From this moment you know him and have seen him."

Philip said, "Lord, let us see the Father and then we shall be satisfied" "Have I been with you all this time, Philip," said Jesus to him, "and you still do not know me?"

"To have seen me is to have seen the Father,
so how can you say, 'Let us see the Father?'
Do you not believe
that I am in the Father and the Father is in me?
The words I say to you I do not speak as from myself:
it is the Father, living in me, who is doing this work.
You must believe me when I say
that I am in the Father and the Father is in me;
believe it on the evidence of this work, if for no other
reason."

(Jn. 14:6-11)

Jesus prepares his friends gently for the pain of his departure. Really one of us, he senses in compassion the ache of inner emptiness that tortures people when a beloved one has passed away. We hurt because of the gap left in our lives. We feel paralyzed because we do not know the way to the place our friend has gone.

Jesus does not want us to be that desperate about his leaving us. He tells us that he is going to a place where we are all called to be: with the Father. He assures us that there is one way to the Father; he is the Way. The depth of this word will never be exhausted. Jesus' last discourse is an invitation to look at him as the mystery of the Way. Every time we ponder this mystery, a new facet lights up for us.

Jesus speaks with love about the beginning and the end of the way: the Father. He insists that to think about the Father meaningfully is to think about him the Son. The opposite is true also: he speaks only about himself as the Son by pointing to his Father. "No one can come to the Father except through me. If you know me, you know my Father too."

To come to the Father, we do not have to travel far and wide. When we know him with heart and soul, when we surrender to him, we are already at our destination; we are already with the Father. To know him is to see in Jesus the mysterious manifestation in the flesh of the Eternal Word. Such is not the knowledge of scholar or student. Knowing him is a graced knowledge of the heart, an embrace of the Spirit. Knowing the Father in him is seeing him in faith. That vision is his gift to us. Only he can make us see the Father in him.

Philip presses Jesus on the promise of vision:

"Lord, let us see the Father and then we shall be satisfied."

How touching is Philip's eagerness to see. Seeing is our first way of becoming acquainted with the people and things around us. Often we have said, when we heard an unbelievable story, "I won't believe it unless I see it." We even have a saying: seeing is believing. I remember when someone told me years ago about a new invention the television. It sounded like pure science fiction. I could not imagine what it would look like before I saw it with my own eyes. No wonder that I, like Philip, long to see the Lord.

The Divine Word became part of the human race. How well he understands our secret longing to see with our own eyes. For he himself was an infant, a child, a young man, an adult who looked with wonder on the world around him. He took it in with love and delight. How well he understands our desire to see the Holy One.

There is only one way in which we may see God here on earth. We cannot see him as we see a friend, a mountain, a glittering stream, sun, stars. For the Father is not created matter as are the persons and things that appear to human eyes. If we would see him in a material way, we would not really see the Father himself, only some pale image of the Infinite. Jesus promises us that he will let us see God as he is once this life is over. It will be a vision that will make us fully share in his glory, a transformed vision that surpasses infinitely our perception of the Divine here on earth. But this is not the seeing-in-faith he speaks about here to his disciples.

"Thank you, Lord, for having created me for this grace of lasting vision, face to face. My deep desire to see you will be fulfilled in a way I cannot even imagine. I understand now that I can only hope here for a shadow of things to come. Give me the grace to experience any view of earthly beauty as pointing to the vision of the Unspeakable that is waiting me: the Beauty of your Being. Let me prepare myself for that divine seeing by deepening in me your gift of faith, hope and love. I accept humbly the limits of the vision of faith here on earth, for this is still the place of pain and temptation, of trust and fidelity, of growth through adversity, of endurance in desperation. I will bear with my longing until you take me up into the mystery of eternal love."

Philip begs Jesus: "Let us see the Father and then we shall be satisfied." He has really understood with the other disciples that the Father is the ultimate satisfaction of the deepest longing of the human heart. Jesus' word and example had shown them daily that the Father is the infinite source from which his life flows forth.

His disciples could not have missed this message. They would have to be blind, deaf, mute, without mind and feeling not to have been touched by Jesus' loving trust in the Father. No wonder Philip realizes that this mysterious Father must be the summit of all a person may hope to attain, to taste, to enjoy. No wonder that he longs to see him with his own eyes.

Jesus realizes that his disciples have not yet grasped

that he is the highest possible appearance of the Father among men. He is the presence of the Father in the flesh for all ages to come. His incarnation of the Invisible One will continue in space and time. He is the everlasting presence of God in mankind and its history. We must not try to find the Father outside of him. God has expressed himself once and for all in Jesus. If we pass him by, we miss the divine light that came into the world. We will dwell in darkness and despair. We will be like a mole that does not know the light it is missing.

"I believe you, Lord. Many seekers have eagerly tried to grow to some vision of the Divine. They have developed countless ways of asceticism and mysticism. They have reached some peace and spiritual satisfaction; they preached their ways to numerous disciples. Yet their ways are limited. You are the only way. Outside of you, the highest experience of the Divine is impossible to attain. It is a pure gift of faith granted to us stumbling mortals because of your life, suffering and death.

"You have lifted many of these travellers to the light. But it was only you who did it, Lord. No amount of human mortification or mysticism can do it alone."

"Philip, who sees me, sees the Father." Everything in Jesus' life—his words and movements, his interests and labors, his meeting with people—are an expression of his humanity as son of Mary and adopted son of Joseph. He is also in every detail of his life the expression of God. He is "the image of the unseen God." (Col. 1:15)

"Have I been with you all this time,
Philip," said Jesus to him, "and you still
do not know me? To have seen me is to have seen
the Father, so how can you say, 'Let us see the
Father?' Do you not believe that I am in the
Father and the Father is in me?"

"Now, Lord, you begin to speak about the kind of
seeing possible for us on earth. You use the word
*believe*. Our seeing is a believing that you are in the
Father and that the Father is in you. It is a vision of
faith, a seeing in darkness."

"The words I say to you I do not speak as from myself:
it is the Father, living in me, who is doing this work.
You must believe me when I say
that I am in the Father and the Father is in me;
believe it on the evidence of this work, if for no other
reason."

Jesus' words carry the presence and the power of the
Father. They touch the human heart; they move the
spirit. When we listen in stillness, they may transform
our hearts and minds. We begin to sense that his
words are welling up from a silent spring of infinite
clarity and depth. Jesus does not speak to make an
impression, to outdo his opponents, to gain power, to
be popular and sought after by the crowd. Never did
he seek his own honor. In every word, he is the envoy
of the Light, the ambassador of the Divine. His words
are filled with unspoken mystery. To unearth their
hidden treasures, we have to abide by them, to ponder

them in our hearts, to taste them. We should stay
faithful to his words even in the midst of aridity. For
then it pleases him to test our faithfulness.

"Your words, Lord Jesus, will not pass away. They
quiet heart and mind, gentle will and passion, give
rise to spontaneous prayer of the heart. To taste your
words, I must listen in a receptivity that quiets my
aggressive mind. I should foster a prayerful openness
to the mystery that hides itself in your words. I must
listen to you in childlike wonder, ready to be surprised
by unexpected light and inspiration.

"Each time I dwell on your words in such docility,
they may yield new treasures. Exposure to your words
is like exposure to the radiance of the sun. Just as the
tree begins to blossom in sunlight, so does the tree of
our divine life begin to blossom in our awareness and
action when we are exposed to the light of your words.

"Next to your words, Lord, are your works, your
deeds. First of all, your miracles. Like your words,
they are important as manifestations of the presence
of the Father in you. What a marvelous
correspondence between your speaking and doing.
Words and works clarify each other, sustain and stay
in tune with one another. To see this harmony
between your words and deeds sustains my faith,
Lord. It helps me to see the Father shining forth in
you."

When we meditate on these words and works, we
are touched at times by light: We *see* a little. Ours is a
seeing within faith, a seeing that springs from and in
turn deepens faith. Prayerfully present to Jesus' words

and deeds In a beginning faith, we may suddenly experience, that is, *see* the divine mystery that lights up in them. This view gives rise to a deeper, more complete believing. This vision of the mystery of God in Jesus' words and deeds is one of the gifts we make ourselves ready for in the spiritual life. He grants it to us if we, in patient and prayerful openness, meditate on the scriptures.

Spiritual life is a tension between seeing and believing. Jesus and the Father "see" each other eternally. Jesus' highest joy is that intimacy of divine vision. He wants us to enter into that mystery of intimacy. For he has said: " . . . so that where I am you may be too." (Jn. 14:3)

To be where Jesus is, is to share in some measure the vision of his Father. This vision begins already on earth. We are invited by Jesus to see the Father in him, the Son. We are called to see the inscrutable in the mirror of creation. The height of this creation is the humanity our Lord assumed. In him, you and I are called to reconcile with the Father all of creation, all of humanity, all that is earthly, temporal and passing. To heal and complete his broken creation is the meaning of our Christian life.

# XI

## WORKING WITH JESUS

"I tell you most solemnly
whoever believes in me
will perform the same works as I do myself,
he will perform even greater works,
because I am going to the Father.

(Jn. 14:12)

Jesus promises us that we may do the same works as
he did here on earth. Our daily action is no longer our
action alone. Our tasks should all be a participation in
his action in the world.

Even more surprising, our works may be greater
than his. What a touching manifestation of his
dynamic presence in history, in the activity of us, his
friends and followers. He means what he says. He
begins his promise with the words, "I tell you most
solemnly." That is, he puts himself, with his whole
power, authority and love, behind this promise.

"Whoever believes in me will perform the same
works as I do myself." Most impressive were his
miracles. Yet we should not limit ourselves to them

alone. We should think about all his deeds, even the most simple ones.

All Jesus' works were done to please the Father. His miracles were only highlights at the end of his life. He did them to glorify the Father and to help people believe in his mission. Yet all his other actions were as much a glorification of God as his miracles.

His daily play as a child in Nazareth, his manual work, his interaction with the people of his village, his travelling and preaching—all were done to fulfill his Father's will. He never went beyond the limits the Father allowed him. He accepted the boundaries of his country town, the restrictions of his people, the limitations of his culture and religion. He tolerated the faults of his disciples. His only striving was to be in harmony with the mission of the Father. It was not his ambition to perform as many miracles as possible so as to evoke surprise and wonder in people. Most of his deeds were not miracles. They were simple and common, as are our deeds in daily life. Yet because they were the work of God, they had infinite meaning and value.

Silent deeds can be more important than miracles. We must allow the silence of Jesus to live on in us, to perform in us the work of God in its totality, in every detail. The decisive thing in our life is to find out how he wants to work in us.

"I understand, Lord, that only one thing is important: to do the work you give me. You want to live in me in a special way. This way is the work of my life as a whole, a work assigned to me by the Father. I don't know yet what my life direction is supposed to be in its totality. This is a mystery hidden in you. My life, like yours, will unfold itself out of many daily actions.

"You want me to appraise, in the light of the Spirit, each little task that comes my way. If more tasks offer themselves to me, I must select the one most in keeping with the direction your Spirit gives me. I may not see where all these works lead. They may seem to be without connection.

Sometimes they all look insignificant. Yet I believe that no work done in your name is without value. It is you doing in me all these little things for the sake of the Kingdom. You weave all these small strands together into one marvelous tapestry: the mysterious whole of my divine life direction.

"This little life of mine is elevated immensely. In you, I am performing the work of the Lord. It does not matter how simple my work may be. I can never wish to have done something greater with my life than doing your work."

If we believe in him, if we live and work in faith, we are already doing his works. We become more and more at one with our Lord. Out of this oneness flow forth the true works of God. He asks us to lend him our eyes to see, our mouth to speak, our ears to hear, our mind to think, our heart to love, our feet to walk, our hands to act. He wants to use us to foster the kingdom of God.

The visible reach of the work of Jesus' followers is far wider than his was at that moment in history. He is with all of us until the end of time. He travels in his followers through all ages. During his life, it was his Father's will that he would restrict his work within the borders of Israel. The Father allowed him only a small number of disciples. The time of his public apostolate was less than three years. His brief, intense life was meant to be the beginning of the greater works of God to be done by the men and women who would follow him. He manifested his generous power and grace in Peter, his apostle. His Spirit made it possible for Peter to gain three thousand new believers in his first sermon. This shows what he meant by greater works.

Jesus planted the seed; his disciples are called to bring in the harvest. Our work is his work. He did not want to do the work of God alone. He lives on in solidarity with the human race of which he became a member. He invites every human being to join him in the work of God.

There will come a time when the participation of each member of his body will be brought to light. Magnificent and simple participations—all will be recognized by our Father in heaven. At that moment of truth, we will see how all these works are linked together in the mysterious history of salvation.

Let us not, then, be fascinated only by works that seem impressive. No one knows what is great in the eyes of God. We must never lose our peace of mind by being concerned about the greatness of the work we are doing. We need to ask ourselves only, "Am I doing the work of God?" and then try to live in obedient openness to his will. Only then can we hear the whisper of his Spirit in our heart. We develop, then, a fine radar for works that are in tune with the direction his Spirit gives to our lives.

"Lord, I have understood that I am called to do the works of God, that each one of us is called to a special work in this life. To know my tasks, I must listen to your Spirit in me. The Spirit may speak in a revelation, but this is an exception. The regular way in which he addresses me is to speak first of all in my own make up, my body, my psyche, my human spirit. He speaks in my background, my expertise and my skill. He speaks in my interests and affinities. Your Spirit speaks in the situation in which I am living. Many works of God, many hobbies, jobs and lifestyles are appropriate for others but are clearly not for me.

"Teach me, Lord, to listen to God's will speaking in my temperament, disposition and past history. If I were to choose a work of God not meant for me, I would harm the spread of your kingdom. Teach me to appraise the life situation you have placed me in. What can I, as this unique person in Christ, do best in the situation in which God has inserted me?

"This dialogue with my situation unfolds in the light of your Spirit. Through it, you disclose to me what the Father wants of me so that I may grow to the fullness of my life direction.

"You want me to keep in touch with your Father's will speaking in my past when making up my mind about his works to be done here and now. I must take into account the works I have already done in my life. They may disclose the direction you want me to take

now. Central in my dialogue is not only a discovery of
what I am called to do here and now, of what I was
called to do in my past; I must also take into account
your reaching out in me to what I may become in the
future in faithfulness to the tasks assigned to me by
your Father.

"When I discover the works to be done and when I
am faithful to this discovery, a new me will emerge out
of the doing of them. You make me a new creation in
ways I could not foresee. In and through my daily
work, you are reaching out to what I am not yet but to
what I am called to become in your mystical body."

The call to the works of God appears everywhere.
First of all, in us; then in everything he inspires us to
do. We must catch his inspiration at work in
ourselves. We must find the whisper of his Spirit at
the root of our best thoughts, feelings, and actions.

Each time we come to him as the originating source
of our spiritual action, mood and reflection, we
are faced with a manifestation of his presence in us.
We can rest in him. We can participate quietly in his
presence at the base of what we think, feel and do. We
do not feel lonely there. We flow with him, the
mysterious power of the Divine. We find the strength
and inspiration to seek out anew the works of God
destined for us from eternity.

We do not find the divine call to work in ourselves
alone. Our graced self in turn reaches out to all things
in life that may contain a hidden invitation to action.
In some sense, these outward invitations to work for
his kingdom are an extension of our graced self. Our

graced self direction includes our whole inner and outer world. Everywhere in that world the Spirit of Jesus is speaking.

"Lord, enable me to distance myself from inner agitation. Agitation silences the voice of the Spirit. It makes me less able to appraise my daily situation. Agitated work is not your work, Jesus. Agitation devours the energy you have given me to perform peacefully the works of the Lord. I work outside the realm of your presence. I become tired, irritable, less effective. Not doing—in and with you—the works of God, I cease to grow as a unique member of your body. To let you work in me enhances my capacity to know, to achieve, to enjoy; it recharges my vital energy; it renews my spirit. Such graced work fills a void felt by people everywhere. Working in and with you, Jesus, is a simple way of communion with the Father."

This way of divine work is the way to the Kingdom Jesus spoke about. If we discover it and strive to live it, he will radiate his peace in our actions. This peace of union with Father's will may fill the atmosphere around us.

The Spirit of Jesus usually speaks to us in ordinary ways. He may speak in a way that is out of the ordinary, though this is an unusual event. It would be foolish to wait for such a thing to happen. We must never wait for an extraordinary message from the beyond, for, in the meantime, we may remain deaf to the whisperings of his Spirit in our daily life.

Led by the Spirit, we must look peacefully at daily

life, its beauties and demands. We must be sensitive
to the people around us. We must look at ourselves—
our strengths and deficiencies, our past and personal
history—and be present to all of these dimensions in
prayer. Then the Spirit may reveal to us the works we
should do in Jesus and how to do them. To know the
path our Father wants for us and to follow it faithfully
will fill us with serenity.

Remember how Jesus rejoiced in gratefulness that
his Father had made known to the little ones what was
hidden from the great and wise. Only the humble find
out what God wants them to do with their lives. If we
are truly humble in him, we will no longer harbor
longings for what we cannot be, for works we cannot
do. Such longings are a hindrance to the life of the
Spirit. They make it difficult for us to find the works
of God in the only place we can find them: in our daily
life with others.

These are the works that are really ours. All other
kinds of work may sound interesting, exciting, more
fulfilling. Our Father may not want them for us.

Deep down, we may not really give up the works he
asks us to sacrifice. We are secretly preoccupied with
tasks that cannot be ours. They sap our energy. We do
not allow him to be wholly present in us to the daily
tasks demanded of us. His Spirit enlightens us only
when we are reading the book of everyday life in
reverence and surrender.

Longing for works that cannot be ours is an obstacle
to our growth in Jesus. Such longing strikes at the root
of his life in us. Blinded by preoccupation with tasks

not meant for us, we cannot discover what the will of the Father is in our daily life. We lose track of what our unique life in Jesus should be.

The temptation to do some other work than what we are called to is always there. We may begin to live in fantasy what we cannot live in day-to-day reality. We become alienated from ourselves, estranged from the will of the Father. We live in deception.

Remember Jesus' temptations in the desert. The temptor promised him kingdoms, status, acclaim, nourishment—service from angels if he would give up the work his Father asked him to do. As a young boy, he went with his parents to the temple in Jerusalem. His heavenly Father wanted him to stay behind with the learned men in the temple. His distraught mother finally found him. She reproached him. At that moment, he felt the pull of the simple wish of a child to be like other children. It pained him to have saddened his mother. Yet he had to do the work of the Father as he wanted it done at that moment. He told her that he had to be about the things of his Father.

Remember the temptation to escape Father's work that came from his own friends and disciples. He hinted to them that the work of his Father would bring him pain and lead to a shameful death. Some tried to dissuade him from this path. They tried to win him over to their anxious wish that he should engage in less dangerous activities. As a human being, he felt tempted to do what they begged him to do. It was as if Satan tried to take him away from the work of God. In anguish, he beseeched his disciples to go away from him. He even called one of them "Satan." He told his disciples that they only understood the works of man; they were impervious to the works of God he had to perform at any price.

Remember at the end of his life, that evening in the Garden: the temptation again presented itself. Look at the other more quiet and pleasant works he could perform if he only would stay alive. In agony, he cried out to the Father: Take away the chalice of suffering, change the work of pain and death you ask of me. Yet he affirmed his faithfulness to his life direction as it had to be in the design of his Father: Not my will but yours be done.

"Lord, how grateful I am for your example. You became like us in everything but sin. Like you, I should resist every temptation to leave the simple tasks you want for me. You not only gave me your example; you also gave me your Spirit as a source of insight, a spring of action.

"My culture places a premium on achievement. It fosters excessive competition. We try to outdo friends and neighbors. This stand takes us away from your peace. I exert myself beyond the limits your Father has granted me. My work becomes oppressive, all encompassing. It makes painful demands; it engulfs me."

Over-exertion is the opposite of what happens when we do the work of God. Working for our Father is a matter of relaxed tuning into his will. When we discover what he wants us to do, we do it in love and in peace. We quietly accept ourselves; we peacefully overcome resistances; we avoid over-exertion as much as laziness.

When Jesus came into the world, he expressed the whole meaning of his life in these words: "I said, as is written of me in the book, I have come to do your will O God." (Heb. 10:7) This attitude shaped his life of work; it directed his movement and inspired his thoughts, feelings, and deeds. His life of work was a song of praise to the Father, a joyful abiding by his will.

"None of those who cry out, 'Lord, Lord,' will enter the kingdom of God but only the one who does the will of my Father in heaven." (Mt. 7:21) "Whoever does the will of my heavenly Father is brother and sister and mother to me." (Mt. 12:15)

Jesus did only the works that pleased his Father. "The one who sent me is with me. He has not deserted me since I always do what pleases him." (Jn. 8:29) "Doing the will of him who sent me and bringing his work to completion is my food." (Jn. 4:34)

Jesus said to his parents who were searching for him in sorrow when he stayed behind in the temple, "Why did you search for me? Did you not know I had to be in Father's house?" (Lk. 2:49) ". . . but the world must know that I love the Father and do as the Father has commanded me. Come, then! Let us be on our way." (Jn. 14:31) Then in the Garden, suffering the agony of his coming passion and death, he prayed three times: "My Father, if it is possible, let this cup pass me by. Still, let it be as you would have it, not as I." (Mt. 26:39) He remained faithful to the Father's work until his last moment. ". . . obediently accepting even death, death on a cross!" (Ph. 2:8)

"I see from your life, my Lord, that there is no greater act of worship than fidelity to the work of God. This faithfulness should be my main concern. I should seek first the work God wants me to do in my life. All the rest will then be given to me. I do not have to be concerned, for my fidelity to you cannot outdo your fidelity to me."

Even from eternity our Father has seen each life in its smallest detail. "No hair falls from your head without his knowledge." (Mt. 10:30) All changes of work that may emerge and disappear in our life, like the rising and falling waves of the sea, have been allowed by our Father, not in indifference but in concern. "We are truly his handiwork, created in Christ Jesus to lead the life of good deeds which God prepared for us in advance." (Ep. 2:10) We may not comprehend always why he wants this or that work to be done by us. "How deep are the riches and the wisdom and the knowledge of God! How inscrutable his judgements, how unsearchable his ways! For who has known the mind of the Lord? Or who has been his counselor?" (Rm. 11:43-45)

"Thank you, Lord, for telling me about your concern for me. Deep inside I may feel that nobody can be more concerned about me than I myself. Yet your love for me is so much deeper than my love for myself; you take my interest to heart much more than I could ever do. With infinite care, you take into account the most hidden aspects of my life. Your loving attention penetrates into the secret needs of my personality, needs unknown even to myself. The works you allow in my life flow forth from your love for me."

Clearly, there is no greater thing we can do than to be faithful to the work of God in the most simple events of our daily life. We must do the common work of every day in an uncommon way—doing this work in loving union with Jesus. It may sometimes seem easier to do great things than to do small ones. The grandeur of an enterprise, the excitement of a splendid project, the interest of others carries us forward. Their admiration sustains us in such moments more than Jesus' grace. We act, then, not because of him but because we feel successful, important, liked, needed. We become spellbound by praise, so much so that we no longer hear his voice in the depth of our hearts. Bewitched by the projects of people, we become estranged from the Father's work. Spoiled by success, we may become alienated from him.

We ought never to forget that true union with Jesus shows itself most in faithfulness to the Father's work in the smallest events. Many of these works cannot give us recognition from others. Most of them are too small to be noticed.

The nature of the task to which we are called by the Spirit is not that important. Our performances may be great or small, hidden or public, humble or exalted. It does not matter. The only thing that counts is that the Eternal wills it. There is no need for further concern. What matters is our surrender to God's work.

"Thank you, Lord, for this wisdom. Help me to be

faithful in little things. If I am called to greater works, remind me that the path of greatness is not the safest path for men. Remind me that the best preparation for fidelity to uncommon works is faithfulness in the common works of everyday life."

If we ever doubt this truth, recall that Jesus spent most of his life as an unknown laborer in a forgotten village. His fellow townsmen were astounded to the point of indignation when at the end of his life, he began to speak up in public. Irritated, they asked each other: "Is that not the son of the carpenter whose father and mother we know?" When Jesus kept appearing in public, they sincerely thought that he must have gone mad. In genuine concern, they tried to bring him back home where they hoped he would calm down and take up again the everyday chores he was accustomed to. He had been so faithful to the common work of everyday life that they could not imagine how he could ever be called to greater works.

The Lord spent only a few years in public life. Even then he went away at times to hide himself from the people. He chose the simple life for most of the time that he walked on earth. Think of the marvelous books he could have written, the astounding art he could have created, the political wonders he could have performed as a social leader of a racial minority of Jews in the Roman Empire. He could have excelled as a foreign missionary instead of insisting on only working for the abandoned souls in his home country, the House of Israel.

Think of the housing projects he, as a master

craftsman, could have developed for the poor in the cities like Jerusalem. Think of what he could have done for the countless underprivileged in the Roman state. He could have been a successful social agitator for human rights; he could have rallied the slaves of the empire into a massive fight for liberation. All these works would have been noble and important, but they were not Father's will for him. Instead, he passed almost all of his life as an unnoticed worker in a forgotten country town.

"Thank you, Lord, for choosing to live most of your life in the routine of everyday labor. You have given me an example of the way in which I can sanctify myself if I am called to the quiet of a simple life. You have given me an example of a day-to-day spiritual life lived within the limits of an unpretentious situation.

"I know, my Lord, that countless works can be done for you. But out of all these works, you in your love want only certain works to be done by me. You alone know the works that will be mine. You reveal these works to me step by step. I cannot know, as you, how each work is linked to the work before and to the works you will ask me to do hereafter. Sometimes I lose my path, but you always wait for me with infinite patience. You are the shepherd who returns me steadily to the pasture of my own work. Help me to be present in the simplicity of my heart to each work along the way you have laid out for me."

## XII

## PRAYING IN JESUS

"Whatever you ask for in my name I will do, so that the Father may be glorified in the Son. If you ask for anything in my name, I will do it." (Jn. 14:13-14)

The Lord's promise in this passage is tremendous in its amplitude and assurance. He does not say it once; he reiterates it with great emphasis. It is as if he is concerned that we would not really count on it. It is as if he understands our surprise. We are of such little faith and his promise seems so sweeping we cannot believe he meant it truly. It sounds to us like an exaggeration, a pious metaphor, a rhetorical exclamation. And yet, he assures us he means every word of it.

"Lord, forgive my doubt. So often I have prayed for things, but I did not obtain what I asked for. Even if some of what I asked was granted to me, it seemed meager and disappointing in the light of your promise. Often what I received was not what I was led to expect when reading your generous words. I was told by you to ask and I would receive. I have asked often and was left empty-handed. You have said: Seek and you will find. I sought and nothing came of it."

We have been disappointed because we did not know what prayer is in his name and for the glory of the Father. He said, "Whatever you ask for in my name, I will do, so that the Father may be glorified in the Son." What we ask can only be granted when it enhances his Father's glory and when we ask the Father in his name.

"Forgive me for being so ignorant. I often asked for what I foolishly imagined would help your cause and would foster my life for you in this world. In your wisdom and kindness, you did not grant me all my prayers. Sometimes you let me see later that the granting of my request would have been harmful to myself and to your kingdom. Often I may not discover why you thought it wiser not to give me what I was asking for. My belief in you must be deep enough to trust that it somehow was not good for me to receive what I desired so strongly. I should realize that I can never know the hidden history of your kingdom and the mystery of my role in its unfolding. The coming of the kingdom and my place in it will remain a mystery during my lifetime. I cannot know what is best for me and for your sake. Therefore, I cannot always know what I should ask for in prayer."

In this way Jesus' Spirit may enlighten us about his promise. We know that he supports us in this world with all his divine resources, with all the grace and power of his Father. They cannot fail. With his always present power, we can do anything and everything that God may ask of us. We pray that we may know what to pray for. We pray as best as we can, with as much faith and confidence as we will be graced with. We are convinced that even though we are praying for something he cannot give us for our own good, something else will be given instead much better for us in the long run. For there is no prayer in his name that goes unheard. In some mysterious way, all prayers of all people are fulfilled.

In his first promise, Jesus tells us that we would do the same works he would do and even greater ones. In the second promise, he says that anything we ask will be granted to us if we ask in his name and if it glorifies the Father. In between these two promises, he says, "because I am going to the Father." His going to the Father is the secret source of both promises. His going does not mean that he is taken away from this world. Since his resurrection, he is in the midst of humanity. He dwells always among us as a divine presence of power and love. Going to the Father means that he will now exercise also in his glorified humanity the divine power that is his from eternity with his Father. As long as he lived a human life on earth, he chose to abstain in his humanity from the full manifestation of his divine power. He emptied himself, becoming one of us, a humble man living a limited life.

This emptying was part of his obedience to the Father. But now the glory and the power of the Father will become fully manifest in his glorified humanity. They are no longer hidden. Now his holy humanity will work for all of us without any restrictions. Since his incarnation and resurrection, he works and prays in the name of us. We work and pray in turn in his name.

"I see, Lord, that I should pray in your name. I must pray as if you were praying in me. Every time something seems important for my life, for the Kingdom, I pray to the Father to give it to me in you and because of you. Yet I realize now that you know my situation better than I ever could. You know solutions I cannot dream of. Therefore, I give you a free hand. Never again will I try to bind you to my prayer, to the one solution I have in my small mind.

Also, my Lord, let me not pray that I may be relieved from all possible effort or pain in the work for your Kingdom. That would not really be praying in your name and in your Spirit. To pray in your name means that I am ready to accept suffering as you accepted yours. Praying in your name and in your Spirit, Jesus, means that I am not only thinking about myself. Implicit in my prayer must always be a silent invitation to God to enlist me in his service—a readiness for anything he asks me to do."

In this way, our prayer becomes really Jesus' prayer and he assures us that if we pray in his name and if what we ask for serves the glory of the Father, it will always be given to us. We can be sure that if it is not given, something far better will be granted in its place. If we live in this climate of surrender, our prayers will be fulfilled. We will not be afraid to ask for anything we feel in need of; even our most vital and human needs may give rise to prayer. Nothing of the things we need are too unimportant for our loving Father. As long as any of our needs and desires—also the earthly ones—can be fulfilled without harming his greater glory, he will grant us this fulfillment.

He taught his disciples to pray the "Our Father". Meditate on this prayer. It is a prayer wholly in his name and in his Spirit. In the "Our Father" he glorifies his Father. He asks for his kingdom and he helps us to ask for all the things we need, even for our daily bread. His "Our Father" is the model of all our prayers.

When we pray in Jesus and with Jesus, we will always be in harmony with the Father and the Father with us. There is no separation between Father and Son. We may pray to the Father in the name of Jesus or we may pray to him directly. The Father can grant our prayer in honor of the Son. Or the Son may give us what we ask in honor of the Father. Between Father and Son is perfect unity and harmony: the harmony of divine love. This unity of love continues in the relationship between Jesus and us, his disciples.

Jesus has promised to work and to pray in us. These two promises form a unity. There is a unity between doing the works of God and being listened to by him when we pray. In some way, it is really the same: to do the works of God and to have our prayers answered. Our prayers will be answered because we are doing daily the works of God. And we do the works of God because our prayers are answered. We must never imagine that we can do any work for him without his grace, power and love.

That grace is given to us because of our prayerful attitude. We should not only pray when we sit down in church or chapel or in the quiet of our room or while we walk in the beauty of nature. We must live always in an attitude of prayer. That attitude should be ours even when we are involved in our work in daily life. It is an attitude in the back of our minds, in the depth of our hearts. It is a silent knowledge that without him we can do nothing for the glory of God. It is a profound awareness of our nothingness before his allness. It is a deep faith that he alone can raise each one of our deeds to a divine height. It is a humble conviction that no work for the kingdom is due to us alone. Every graced enterprise flows from us as rooted in him, as sustained by him, as vitalized by his presence.

"Yes, Lord, I am always and everywhere surrounded by your Risen Presence. I move, work and am in you all the time. I can never escape your presence, Lord Jesus. I can only refuse it. I can deny you, Source of my prayer and work. I may try vainly to pray and work in my name only. I may be so foolish as to evoke prayer experiences, even mystical ones, by merely human exercises. They may lead to some pleasant inner experience, even to a natural mysticism. But it is not you praying in me, Jesus. It only cements me more in my own self-sufficiency, in my spiritual arrogance. Without you I will experience a bitter feeling of loneliness.

"The same holds for the works I do. I am so inclined to work agitatedly, thinking that by myself alone I can do everything. That I, by my own power, have to make over the world. Yet sooner or later I will feel frustration, loneliness and disappointment. All work will only partly accomplish what I hoped to attain. Not working in and with you, I cannot live in the hope that the failures of my work may be silently complemented by your loving ongoing activity at the heart of humanity."

Jesus is everywhere at play in this world. We must look at all things as flexible and open to his hand. Nothing is fixed forever. The Lord can give a new form to everything. If we pray in him, he creates with us a state of possibility, of flexibility.

Prayer melts the fixity of our situation. It opens new avenues, new possibilities. One of the gifts of prayer is the revelation of new openings for creative action. A second gift is the grace to do the works necessary to make these new beliefs come true. Prayer makes us infinitely powerful because it is the key to the heart of God and to the sources of human history.

All things are created in Jesus' image. Therefore, all people, events and things present themselves always before the Father as a field of possibilities. There is one key that opens the way to the interior of the world. The key is that what we ask in his name, he will do.

# XIII

## LIVING WITH THE SPIRIT OF JESUS

"If you love me you will keep my commandments.
I shall ask the Father,
and he will give you another Advocate
to be with you for ever,
that Spirit of truth
whom the world can never receive
since it neither sees nor knows him;
but you know him,
because he is with you, he is in you."

(Jn. 14:15-17)

"I have said these things to you
while still with you;
but the Advocate, the Holy Spirit,
whom the Father will send in my name,
will teach you everything
and remind you of all I have said to you."

(Jn. 14:25-26)

The discourse is a reverberation of early Christian reflections on the spirituality of our Lord. The Spirit himself guided John's written expression of these meditations. He safeguarded the final version so that it would not betray the vision of Jesus.

Our spiritual life is deepened by pondering this discourse. Soon we become aware of the recurrence of its themes. This spirituality is not a logical system of syllogisms; it is more like a musical composition. The composer tries to inspire the listener by the repetition of themes. Each time the same melody is played in a different setting, it is blended with other elements. Gradually the listener grows into the movement of the composition. The recurrence imprints the themes in his soul. He begins to flow with it—if not on first listening, then in later ones, provided he is attentive and gently docile.

The same is true of the spirituality of this discourse. Some themes keep reappearing, yet they are set in new contexts that give them added depth. They highlight other aspects of the same loving communication of the Master.

Faithful pondering of the spirituality of Jesus will allow us to flow with these themes, to become truly at home with them until they become life themes.

One of these is the promise of the Spirit. In this first part of the discourse, we find two of the five promises of a new helper. Separated by only a few verses, their content is closely related. Later in the discourse, in Chapter Sixteen, we will meet again the theme of the Spirit and his role in our life. But the content of these later promises seems less related to those we find here.

The Lord at the last supper tells his disciples he is leaving but that they are to do his works, to dwell on his words, to keep his commandments. This is more than a human task, impossible without help from the Holy. Therefore, when Jesus is gone, he will give another helper, the Spirit, to be with them.

The Spirit will carry on the ministry of Jesus. He will not be visible to us as Jesus was to his disciples. He will instead abide with us by a mysterious indwelling in our human spirit. He will remain with us forever. Jesus does not mean that we have two presences in us: his and that of the Spirit. It is one and the same event. Jesus returns to his Father. After his return he himself abides in us through the Spirit.

The real gift of Easter is the possibility of our lasting union with Jesus in spite of his bodily absence. This presence of Jesus in his Spirit is the foundation of our spiritual life. It is promised to all of us, not only to mystics and saints, provided we keep the commandments of Jesus out of love for him.

This Spirit will teach us everything. He will not necessarily teach us more than Jesus did, as if his teachings were incomplete. He will help us to grasp the full meaning of what the Lord already revealed. He will also assist us in finding out what the teaching of the Lord means for us in terms of our own life direction. His promise reminds us of Psalm 25:5: "Guide me along the way of your truth and teach me."

The mission of the Spirit is to complete Jesus' mission in the community of Christians and in our personal lives. The Holy Spirit does not bring us another or a better spirituality than Jesus. He only wants to make Jesus himself more deeply known to us:

his person and his teachings. (Jn. 16:13;15:26; I Jn. 4:1-6, 13-16)

The Spirit has no Gospel of his own. He inspired the evangelists to write the Gospel of Jesus and he keeps assisting the community of Christians over the centuries to disclose the treasures contained in this Gospel. The Spirit is the great reminder of the words of Jesus. His reminding is often filled with light and consolation. Even the Apostles who had heard Jesus himself speak to them were surprised by his light. They discovered in these words a depth and wealth they did not suspect at the time they were spoken. For them too, the sayings of Jesus light up with new significance in the light of the Spirit. (Jn. 12:22; 12:16, 13:7)

We see in the Acts of the Apostles how the Christian community felt about this promise of Jesus. Nothing important was said or done without the assistance of his Spirit. (Acts 16:7) No wonder the Acts are sometimes called the Gospel of the Holy Spirit.

The Spirit is thus really with me and in me. The Lord has told me so. He illuminates my spirit. He is always with me no matter where I go. He accompanies me no matter what troubles me or what I feel. He is there. I find in myself the ramifications of self centeredness. But this is not all. The Spirit is also there. I am not left an orphan by Jesus. His Spirit has become my father and mother. He keeps bringing Jesus to life in me and me in Jesus.

"Thank you, Lord for giving us another helper. You call him a better one than you because you leave your disciples while your Spirit remains with us. He gives you back to us in a new and lasting way. You call him the Spirit of Truth."

Truth in this Gospel means the full reality of the Holy One, his glorious Being. It reminds us of what John proclaims in the beginning of his Gospel: "The Word was made flesh, he lived among us, and we saw his glory, the glory that is his as the only Son of the Father, full of grace and truth." (Jn. 1:14-15)

"Truth" expressed the highest gifts Jesus granted us. Words like grace, truth, life, light, love carry the same ultimate meaning. "The Spirit of Truth" is not so different from "the Spirit of Divine love", for truth means in John's Gospel: God's generosity to open up to us what he is, to communicate to us his own life.

"What else, my Lord, is this truth than Divine Love? The Love that makes me be, that delights my heart, that sustains my daily life? God is Love. Your Father expresses the Love-he-is in you, the Son. This is the first and total outflow of Divine Truth or Love. Father and Son express this love fully in the Holy Spirit. This is a second generation of the truth of God's being which is pure love. The Spirit communicates that love of God to creation. He is the outpouring of the love of your Father and of you, his Son. He is a steady outflow of the Divine into creation and into our hearts.

"Your Father is the origin of Divine Love. You, the Son, are the image of this love. The Spirit is the divine communication of this Love to creation.

"You call each of us to continue this outflow of

truth in the world. We are like little streams coming down from you, we are channels of the love that is God. You give us the Spirit to make us into unique expressions of the Love that generated each of us."

Jesus makes us sense that the Spirit is his highest gift. The Spirit gives himself. For he is a Divine Person, not a thing to be given away passively. All the love our Father and Jesus communicate to humanity is given through the Spirit. The Spirit is the Holy One in his infinite generosity, in his boundless self communication. He is divine sharing. He is the self gift of the Holy One in person.

The Lord tells us that the world can never receive the Spirit since it neither sees nor knows him. Knowing him is not head knowledge; it is knowledge of the heart, a subtle sensing, an experiencing of his presence in our lives. It is that quiet awareness of his touch, tender as the morning dew on flowers opening up for the dawn.

This sacred knowledge is not transparent or clear. We should never try to conjure it up willfully, lest we become victims of our imagination. The Spirit is in us as a soft voice, a mild reminder, a quiet whisper. Only when we are recollected, at one with our deepest selves, may we become aware at a graced moment that he abides in us. We may experience his silent presence as a mysterious mood of peace and love. The Holy Spirit is a modest guest. He seldom lets us sense that we are his beloved host. He announces his presence in so subtle a fashion that is difficult to catch if we do not live lives of gentle recollection.

"Holy Spirit, help me surrender to the boundless love you are. You are the pure communication of the Divine. I live in the shadow of a mystery of evil that pervades the culture I share daily with others. This culture may close itself off from you, relying on its own cleverness, power and technique. Often I feel touched by its dream of self sufficiency. At such moments of arrogance I lose the innocence of receptivity.

"Thank you for not allowing my absorption in a worldly life. What is wordly has lost openness to your silent presence. Prevent my encapsulation in this kind of world, less I become blind to you, Spirit of the humble and the lowly. To be swallowed up by the world is to live in sin against you. This sin cannot be forgiven. As long as I persist in my captivity, not the tiniest opening is left for you. Your forgiveness can nowhere touch my wounded soul.

"I am not swallowed yet by worldliness, my Lord, but seduced by its contagion. The fever of human ambition confuses heart and mind. I am less ready to receive out of your fullness. Deepen my experience of your presence. Make me less vulnerable to a worldliness that resists your gentle power."

We ask for a deepening of the experience of the Spirit. If our asking is humble, in surrender to our Father's will, he loves and hears our prayer. We ask for an experience that will render us less vulnerable to this world. He gave it abundantly to the early Christians. Immersed in a pagan world, they needed this consolation. Jesus gives it today to his little flock threatened by a secular world. He grants this experience especially to Christians who begin to tread the path of the life of the Spirit. Later he may withdraw this consolation, lest we attach ourselves to the felt presence of the Spirit.

The Spirit surpasses infinitely all human feeling. We are to love him also when the night of pure faith descends upon us and dulls our senses. We are never to confuse experience of the Spirit with the Spirit himself. His grace can never be experienced directly. Ecstasy, enthusiasm, inner joy are minor gifts. They are neither the Spirit nor grace as such.

Jesus may lead us often into the desert. We ought not to confuse that dryness with the absence of the Spirit. Yet the moment he grants us the gift of experience, we must not despise or withstand it. We leave it to him to infuse or withdraw the sense of his presence. We follow his gentle lead and never try to lead ourselves.

The Lord tells us that the Father will send the Spirit in his name to teach us everything, to remind us of all he told us. We are called to keep Jesus' words as he kept the word of his Father. To keep the words of Jesus is to dwell on them, to be faithful to them in daily life. Out of this dwelling and this fidelity, his words may emerge vividly for us and for others to whom we speak of the Lord.

We are called to live lives of hope and vigilant expectation between the first and the second coming. The Spirit keeps the memory of Jesus alive between these two comings. We cannot read Scripture well, nor the words of the Church or its masters, with the

light of our minds alone. A special light is needed.
That light is the Spirit. To hear his teaching, we must
silence our inner agitation and "center down" in the
still point of the soul. Then the Spirit may reveal to us
that these words are words of infinite depth, that they
can never be exhausted.

Some of these words may hide a more personal
inspiration. Each of us is called to a life direction that
is an original manifestation of Christ in the world.
Any word of Jesus may carry a subtle nuance that only
one Christian can hear the moment the Spirit wants to
communicate it to his humble and docile heart. The
same may happen to a group of Christians, as we
know from the history of orders and congregations, of
communities and families of lay people called to
witness for the Lord.

This communication of the Spirit is always in the
name of Jesus. No opposition exists between the
teaching of Jesus and his Church and that of the
Spirit. The Spirit does not speak in two tongues. Time
and time again Christians have been tempted to
imagine a spirituality of the Spirit different from that
of Jesus. Often, when the devotion to the Spirit rose,
this split threatened Christian spirituality. The Spirit
does not absolve us from listening to the words of
Jesus and his Church. He only helps us to understand
better and to keep alive the teachings of the Lord.

"The Father sends us the Spirit in your name. What
a touching manifestation, Lord, of your oneness with
the Father. You and the Father share the loving will to
communicate divine life to us. The Father has sent

you among us to manifest in a human way the truth of the Holy. The same Father completes through the Spirit what he began in you.

"The Spirit makes certain that your words are not filed away somewhere in my memory. He resurrects your words in me; he brings them to life. He unfolds in me the mystery of your message. Your Spirit makes me taste how in you, in your mission, words and sacraments all goods are already given to us like ripe seeds ready to flower. The Spirit does not bring us a new doctrine or new sacraments but a fresh understanding of your gifts."

Jesus prays for us constantly that we may be faithful to this light. In the work of salvation he has been called to be the first and the last. The Spirit is sent by the Father as a new mode of communication of the Divine. He has not been sent outside of Jesus. With the cooperation of Spirit, Jesus was brought into this world. It was Jesus' calling to make the divine truth visible and audible in human flesh. He had to prepare the way for the Spirit.

Jesus is and remains the beginning, the middle and the end of the ways of God. He is the beginning: "In the beginning was the Word. . . through him all things came to be." (Jn. 1:1-3) The end: "I am the Alpha and the Omega, the First and the Last, the Beginning and the End." (Rev. 21:13-14) "The Spirit and the Bride say, 'Come'." (Rev. 21:17) "The One who guarantees these revelations repeats his promise: I shall indeed be with you soon. Amen; come, Lord Jesus." (Rev. 21:20-21)

When Jesus comes, he will renew the earth. He will hand over to the Father a lost humanity which he brought home. The Spirit will glorify Jesus and this redeemed humanity. But he will not hand humanity over to the Father. This mission belongs to Jesus to the glorious end. Therefore, the Spirit is sent by the Father in Jesus' name. He has been sent to us because of Jesus' prayer; he has been sent only to complete his work.

"You give me an amazing glimpse of the mysterious life of the Trinity, Lord Jesus. Each of the three divine Persons honors each other in the highest way. Each of them does his own work in creation so that all creatures may glorify God by sharing in his glory. My highest aspiration should be to glorify the Father through the Son in the Holy Spirit for ever and ever."

## XIV

## THE COMING OF JESUS

"I will not leave you orphans; I will come back to you.
In a short time the world will no longer see me;
but you will see me,
because I live and you will live.
On that day
you will understand that I am in my Father
and you in me and I in you.
Anybody who receives my commandments and keeps them
will be one who loves me;
and anybody who loves me will be loved by my Father,
and I shall love him and show myself to him."

Judas—this was not Judas Iscariot—said to him,
"Lord, what is this all about? Do you intend to show
yourself to us and not to the world?" Jesus replied:

"If anyone loves me he will keep my word,
and my Father will love him,
and we shall come to him
and make our home with him.
Those who do not love me do not keep my words.

And my word is not my own:
it is the word of the one who sent me."

                                        (Jn. 14:18-24)


The last discourse is meant to be a consolation for
the disciples who must witness Jesus' departure from
this world. Until now the greatest word of consolation
has not been spoken. There has been the promise of a
house with many rooms, of the second coming of
Jesus, of a new mission of the disciples, of the power of
prayer, of the abiding of the Spirit. None of these
promises can dispel their sadness. Without him they
feel like orphans cut off from the source of their life.

The consolation that would make sense to them at
this moment is that he himself would soon be back
with them. That is what he tells them now. "I will not
leave you orphans; I will come back to you. In a short
time the world will no longer see me; but you will see
me. . . (Jn. 14:18-19) They will see him soon after his
resurrection. He will appear to all of them at various
times. But for those who refuse to believe in him, he
will be invisible forever. (Jn. 7:33-36)

He assures them that they will not only see him
but—because he lives in a whole new way—they will
live also through him a new kind of life. He tells them
that this life will enable them to grasp the real
meaning of his glory; they will realize the oneness
between him and the Father (Jn. 10:38) and the
oneness of himself with those who believe in him.

The manifestation of the resurrection does not
restrict itself to the appearances of Jesus shortly after.

The resurrection is the beginning of a new era, a new day in history.

Jesus rises to new life in the midst of humanity and each person is called to share this life abundantly. Jesus speaks about "that day," an expression used by John three times. (Jn. 14:20; 16:23, 26) He points to the day of his lasting presence after the long night lost humanity was living in before his coming. This lasting day will be made possible by "the hour" of Jesus he spoke about in the beginning of his discourse. Jesus' appearances after his resurrection point to that lasting kind of intimate presence among us.

The central event of this new day of humanity will be a sharing in the inner life of Jesus and his Father. Hence the words of the risen Jesus in Mt. 28:20: "And know that I am with you always; yes, to the end of time." The day of resurrection dawns in every person who loves the Lord and manifests this love by the keeping of his commands.

Such real love of the Son appeals to the love of both Father and Son. The loving disciple will then experience the presence in his life of Father, Son and Spirit.

The disciples seem disturbed that Jesus will not show himself to all people. They still dream about an impressive appearance of Christ, as liberator of Israel. Such an appearance would shock people into the recognition that they had been right after all; it would make up for the hurt, humiliation and ridicule they had suffered. They could say: I told you so. Therefore, the anxious question: "Do you intend to show yourself to us and not to the world?"

The deeper meaning of Jesus' showing himself escapes them still. He will reveal himself to his followers by his indwelling. His new being in this world will not startle the world. The glory of the Risen One in those who believe in him will be a hidden glory.

Jesus does not give a straight answer to the question of Judas. He tries again to clarify for them what it really means to see the Father. He repeats the conditions of loving Jesus and keeping his word. He stresses especially the Father's love for all who follow his Son. Because of that love of the Father for them, they will receive the divine indwelling.

Earlier in this Gospel, Jesus had spoken of the Father's love for the world: "God loved the world so much that he gave his only Son." (Jn. 3:16) This incarnation of the Divine Word was an expression of the Father's love for humanity.

God's indwelling, however, is the special expression of his love for those who follow Jesus faithfully. As the prophet Zechariah had promised in the name of Yahweh: "For I am coming to dwell in the middle of you . . ." (Ze. 2:14) John referred to the worship in spirit and truth" (Jn. 4:24) initiated by the hour of Jesus.

"I will not leave you orphans;
I will come back to you." (Jn. 14:18)

This is a tender saying. It shows us that God is very much at home with us. He has slowly made his presence known to the human race. He revealed his nearness in the events of the people of Israel. The greatest event of the self revelation of God as one of us took place in Jesus. God is the intimate lover of each of us; he reveals the depth of his love and tenderness in these words of Jesus.

At times we feel like orphans, lonely, uneasy and fearful. Sometimes we are so tired of working, of thinking, of trying to help ourselves and others. Everything seems unpleasant and confused. It is as if we have lost our home in this world and in the Church. Then we remember the words of Jesus: "I will not leave you orphans." He really cares for us. We are not alone. He assures us: I will come back to you.

"Never leave me an orphan, Lord. What would I do without you? To whom would I go? Often I lost you but as often you came back to me. I left you in indifference but you never left me. I will never cease to be surprised by your eternal return to me, your unfaithful lover."

"In a short time the world will no longer see me;
but you will see me,
because I live and you will live."

(Jn. 14:19)

The Lord speaks here about the few days he will be away from his disciples. He refers also to the longer time of his bodily absence—the time between his resurrection and the last days, the in-between time in which we are called to live. After his resurrection the world—closed off from God—will no longer see him in the way it saw him when he walked among the people, preaching the word and performing his miracles. His new presence on earth will only be visible for those who believe in him and love him. "But you will see me, because I live and you will live."

The glorified Jesus lives in and among us. We keep emerging as new selves in him. This emergence is the deepest possibility of the graced human person.

In this world our experience of Jesus will remain veiled and dim. No ecstasy may be ours, no flash of exaltation, no sudden change of daily ways. We should believe that in the depth of our being he is transforming us steadily.

Think of a stormy sea. Under the murky waters, life teems abundantly. So is it with his life in us. People may notice our faults and sins, our bad temper, loss of equanimity and self control. But Jesus sees the noble will, the faith he puts at the heart of our turbulent life. We must believe that transfiguration happens deep within us long before it may enter hesitantly our awareness.

His grace of transformation is a hidden power more invisible than electricity or magnetic waves. His inner action rarely betrays itself on the surface of our life. At times we may experience strength and peace in the midst of suffering, failure and defeat. We feel surprised, but at that moment we are seeing him.

"Augment my faith in your silent action, Lord. Don't allow me to become rash and impatient, a disappointed Christian who lost his vision. Let me wait in faith for the vision of your glory in all of us no matter how long this vision may be delayed. Make me live by the words of your prophet:

How long, Yahweh, am I to cry for help
while you will not listen;
to cry "Oppression!" in your ear
and you will not save?

Why do you set injustice before me,
why do you look on where there is tyranny?
Outrage and violence, this is all I see,
all is contention, and discord flourishes.

(Hab. 1:2-3)

Then Yahweh answered and said,
"Write the vision down,
inscribe it on tablets
to be easily read,
since this vision is for its own time only:
eager for its own fulfillment, it does not deceive;
if it comes slowly, wait,
for come it will, without fail.

"See how he flags, he whose soul is not at rights,
but the upright man will live by his faithfulness."

(Hab. 2:2-4)

"Diminish my longing for instant perfection, for impressive change and rash reformation. Teach me that fast growth in showy virtue feeds self love and pride. Help me to tolerate strife and discord. Let me bear with failure, with the whispers behind my back, the knowing smile, the rejection by those more

righteous than I. For you are my vision that will not
disappoint, my integrity in the midst of misery, the
resurrection of the ruins of my life."

"On that day
you will understand that I am in my Father
and you in me and I in you.
Anybody who receives my commandments and keeps them
will be one who loves me;
and anybody who loves me will be loved by my Father,
and I shall love him and show myself to him."

This promise of Jesus gives rise to a third question
by a disciple. Like the two former questions, the first
one by Thomas, the second one by Philip, also this
third one of Judas shows the misunderstanding of the
disciples. It gives Jesus the opportunity to announce a
higher self revelation.

Initially Jesus seems only to repeat: If anyone loves
me, he will keep my word and my Father will love him.
But then, almost unnoticed, something new and
exceptional is added: we will come to him and make
our home in him. That "we" means not only Jesus but
also the Father.

"Your Father will come to me. What a surprise, my
Lord! I know that the Father sends you and the Spirit.
But that the Father himself comes and resides in me
with both of you is an unexpected gift."

When we hear that someone is sent, we imagine
that this person must leave the one who sends him.
That is true for people. It is different for the divine
missions that take place within the Holy Trinity. That

the Father sends the Son and the Spirit can never mean that they have to leave the Father. If one of the Divine Persons is somewhere, also the others must be there. It is true they will not be present in the same manner. Each of them is with us in his own way in accordance with his place in the Trinity.

Jesus speaks about the coming of two persons: the Father and the Son. Earlier he spoke about the coming of the Spirit. He thus reveals to us the coming and the indwelling of the Holy Trinity.

This visitation is a mystery that cannot be fathomed. Many saints unfolded their spiritual life in contemplation of this indwelling of the Trinity. They were mindful of this inhabitation in the graced center of their lives.

Jesus even speaks about the homemaking of the Holy Trinity. What is homemaking? A man buys a new house, empty, bare and uninviting. A woman, a homemaker, enters with the magic of her taste and sensitivity. She brings rugs, furniture, paintings; she lights the fire and hangs the lamps. She transforms the house into a home, warm, clean and intimate.

The Holy Trinity is the homemaker of our souls. Before its entrance, our heart was like a cold house without charm and intimacy, dusty and unclean. Since the Trinity entered, this house is transformed into a home; we cooperate with this transformation by keeping the words of Jesus.

"How can I hear this revelation, Lord, and be so indifferent to its truth? My faith is too faint, my love too little, my heart too small.

"Many times a day I repeat: In the name of the Father, the Son and the Holy Spirit. Often it is a routine movement, an empty custom; my heart is not in it; my mind is distracted. I am not truly there.

"Father, Son and Spirit, you are the neglected guests of my soul. Instead of offering you a loving residence, I give you a cheap boarding house whose landlord is mostly far away. Only when I need some favors I may pass by and demand the rent."

The divine guests of our soul may quietly announce to us that they are there. They have come to commune with us. Loving communion is God's very nature. The highest demonstration of this divine communicability is the fact that God exists as a community of three persons. Their communicative presence in us is meant to spread joy and peace in our lives, to lift us beyond the dreariness of everyday, not by freeing us from routine but by granting what we do a new and vital meaning.

The Trinity is in us to intensify and purify our spirit. At times we may experience that the Trinity within makes us surpass the isolated meanings of singular creatures. Suddenly we see the mysterious direction of the universe as a luminous outflow of the love of the Trinity. We sense the harmonious immersion of our own life direction within this flow of eternal love and wisdom that permeates all being.

To recognize the Son in the Father is already a beginning of this graced awareness of the divine presence the Trinity evokes in us.

"Thank you, Lord, for this manifestation of the

Trinity within me. Help me to escape two extremes. One is to attach myself to enlightenment and consolation, to hunt greedily for religious experience. The other is to deny that the Trinity within me may give rise at times to the gift of contemplation.

"Your threefold presence in me is a mysterious, inner reality, infinitely surpassing my consciousness. I can never force your living presence to my awareness. Neither can I compel the grace of illumination. You made the masters of the spiritual life warn me against such willfulness."

Grace is by no means the same as the feeling of God's presence. To believe so would expose us to self deception. In that belief we may become complacent whenever we feel peaceful and devout. Left without this feeling, we might feel depressed and be inclined to despair. We should root our life in faith alone, not in feeling.

Yet we should not fall into the opposite extreme, that is, we should not be so fearful of self deception that we close out any ray of light he may allow to enter our awareness. The Trinity made its home in us to make itself known to us in God's own good time. At times the Divine Persons break their silence and flood our heart with friendliness, love and peace. At such moments we are not any better than we were before. This self manifestation does not mean that the Divine Persons are more present in the core of our soul. It only pleases them to grant us a glimpse of their presence.

"Now I understand what you tried to tell me, Jesus,

in the words: 'On that day you will *understand*' and 'I will *show* myself.' Make me ready to receive any awareness of your presence you may allow in my life. Let me neither underrate nor overrate its meaning. Let me never mistake it as an index of holiness. Let me simply be there graciously any time you want to show yourself to me."

The Trinity who dwells in us does not always withhold the sign of its presence. We cannot always sense the joy of being graced nor can we steadily feel that we are in grace. The Trinity may allow us at times to experience a certain peace as a sign of its gracing presence.

Jesus makes clear to us how this indwelling will happen and what its conditions are. He says: "Who receives my commandments and keeps them" and "If anyone loves me he will keep my word." Only then will the Trinity come to us and make its home with us.

We have to be the keepers of the words of Jesus. We have to carry them with us, to read them, to dwell on them. We must keep his words not only by dwelling upon them; we must let them flow into our whole make-up, our interaction with people, events and things, our participation in history. The commands and words of Jesus should first permeate our memory, mind, will and sensitivity; after that, our daily words, actions and social involvement.

"The more I let this happen, the more your Father will love me, Jesus. The more I keep your word, the more I become that word. The Father, looking at me, sees more and more the Word that is his own Son. I show the Father increasingly your face. Therefore you say: If you love me you will keep my word, and my Father will love you, and we shall come to you and make our home with you.

"You also warn me, Jesus: 'Those who do not love me do not keep my words. And my word is not my own: it is the word of the one who sent me.' (Jn. 14:24)

"The only thing that counts for you is that I love you. The measure of my love is the keeping of your word. How central your word should be in my spiritual life."

Jesus wants us always to remember that his word is not his own; it is the word of the one who sent him. He referred to his Father always during his life here on earth.

Jesus' whole last discourse shows to us how deeply he is filled with the conviction that the words he speaks are not his own. He wants us to live and speak out of the same conviction. Our words are worthless in the realm of the Kingdom. We must give them to Jesus and he shall make them his; they shall then carry the divine power to change hearts. We shall speak with humility, for the words of the proud cannot touch the souls of his people.

We are too sinful to always keep his commandments and to live by his words. Let us never deny our weakness. As his disciple, John, tells us in his first letter: "If we say we have no sin in us, we are deceiving ourselves and refusing to admit the truth . . ." (1 Jn. 1:8)

We are nearest to him when we acknowledge how

much we need him. To say we are sinners is to admit our need. He loves us for that. His grace makes us aware of the gap between what he calls us to be and what we are. His word becomes an admonishment for us. Yet if we love him, we keep dwelling on his word even while it pains and humbles us that we can never keep it perfectly.

The more repentant we are, the more his life in us unfolds itself. The climate of love and humility is the only climate in which the flower of his grace will grow.

## XV

## THE PEACE OF JESUS

"Peace I bequeath to you,
my own peace I give you,
a peace the world cannot give, this is my gift to you.
Do not let your hearts be troubled or afraid.
You heard me say:
I am going away, and shall return.
If you loved me you would have been glad to know that
I am going to the Father,
for the Father is greater than I.
I have told you this now before it happens,
so that when it does happen you may believe.
I shall not talk with you any longer,
because the prince of this world is on his way.
He has no power over me,
but the world must be brought to know that I love the
Father
and that I am doing exactly what the Father told me.
Come now, let us go."

(Jn. 14:27-31)

This first part of the discourse ends as it began with
words of encouragement. Jesus assures the disciples

that a new power will be given to him which will make
it possible for him to dwell even more intimately with
them after his death. As usual his parting word is
"Peace," Shalom. Jesus leaves his *own* peace with
them. It belongs to him alone, but he bequeaths it like
a legacy; he gives it like a treasure.

What he gives is not first of all a feeling of peace.
The peace of Christ is an invisible, graced state of life.
We could compare it with the state of health. We may
or may not feel our health; it is simply a condition of
our organism granted to us by nature. So it is with the
state of peace our soul is graced with by the Lord.

A feeling of good health, of vital well being, may
flow from my healthy condition. Yet this experience of
vitality may be slight, even absent at times. The
reverse holds true too; namely, a person may feel in
excellent shape yet he may not be healthy any longer.
Already a deadly disease may be eating away inside
him.

The same is true of the state of peace Jesus leaves
his followers. It is the condition of reconciliation with
God. The word peace in John is like the words truth,
light, joy. They express facets of the gift of eternal life
that Jesus has brought from the Father. This gift of
life implies a basic state of peace with God.

The fact that a small country is basically at peace
with a mighty neighbor does not imply that all citizens
enjoy daily an elated feeling of peace. They take it for
granted. Feelings are deceptive. Even when the state
of peace is broken because of belligerence between the
two countries, many citizens may falsely feel at ease,

not paying attention to the fact that war may be imminent.

Similarly the full awareness and enjoyment of the state of peace Jesus established between us and the Father is a minor matter. The subjective experience of peace may flow from the state of peace with God Jesus left us as our inheritance. The feeling may come also when we meditate prayerfully on this gift but, even then, we are not always free from discord and agitation. Briefly, the peace Jesus leaves and gives to his disciples means far more than a sense of safety and composure in the face of danger. It speaks about the deepest invisible relation of the disciples to God. This peace is one of the fundamentals of Christian spirituality.

"Do not let your hearts be troubled or afraid." These words are an introduction to the following words of Jesus in which he tells why we should not be afraid. We should not take these words as a further explanation of the peace Jesus just spoke about. For, as we have seen, the peace-offering of Jesus is the gift of a basic state of reunion with God; it may or may not be accompanied by the absence of fear or dismay.

Jesus wants to say here that his going to death should not cause fear and dismay in the hearts of his disciples. They should look forward to the enjoyment of the results of his sacrifice. He shows them once more what his death really means to them and to himself. If they love him at all, they ought to be glad that he has accomplished what his Father asked him to do; that he returns to the Father who is greater than the human Jesus they have thus far known.

"You heard me say: I am going away and shall return." He repeats again one of the leading themes of the discourse: the connection between his departure and his return. If they would only believe in his return, they would even be able to experience joy.

While he is concerned about them, Jesus himself, like all other human beings, wants friendship too. He wants his friends to think not only about their own concerns but also about his feelings and future. So he goes on: "If you loved me you would have been glad to know that I am going to the Father, for the Father is greater than I."

Jesus does not deny that the disciples love him. He gently chides them for a limitation in their love. This limitation is due to their lack of understanding about the meaning of Jesus' death. If their love had been more enlightened, they would have been able to share Jesus' joy about his going to the Father.

He adds that the Father is greater than he is. Jesus sits in lowliness in the midst of disciples who do not understand; waiting for his death, betrayed by one of his own; how deeply he experiences the freely chosen self limitation of his divine powers at this moment. The Father had not assumed any of this temporary dimming of the divine glory. The Father is greater than the human nature of Jesus so vulnerable in this hour. But Jesus will soon return to the Father. All these limits will fall away from him. What a joy this will be for all who love him.

If their love for him had been enlightened, if they

had known their own best interest, they would have been glad to know that his departure would lead to his glorification. Jesus will return to the divine glory that the Word possesses from eternity. The incarnation had dimmed temporarily its radiance. To be sure, the divine glory was present in Jesus' humanity from the beginning but not in its fullness. After his death, however, the glory of the Eternal Word overflows fully the humanity of Jesus. The manifestation of the presence and power of God will break out in his wounded and humiliated body, just as the sun breaks from behind clouds and drenches us in its light. The disciples should rejoice also for their own sake. For in the Lord's humanity, our humanity is glorified. His glorified humanity becomes our gateway to the Holy Trinity, our entrance to the Divine Family.

Salvador Dali has painted our Lord at this last supper. The apostles lie around the table but Jesus stands there, tall and luminous as already risen, uplifted and radiating the mysterious light of his glorification over them and over a new world. The pristine beauty of a new heaven and a new earth is symbolized by the transfigured lake and mountains, fresh and resplendent behind him, and by the cenacle that has become floating and transparent. We could envision the painting as celebrating the new presence of Jesus in our history after he has returned to his Father.

"I have told you this now before it happens, so that when it does happen you may believe." Jesus predicts his death so that when it occurs, his disciples will not be disturbed but will, on the contrary, find a new motivation to believe in him.

"I shall not talk with you any longer, because the prince of this world is on his way. He has no power over me, but the world must be brought to know that I love the Father." He assures them that Satan, the prince of this world, has no power over him no matter what happens. For he is the Son of God and he is without sin. (Jn. 8:46; 16:33; 19:11)

Satan has a certain power over other people. They have consented to this power insofar as they have sinned. Jesus escapes his negative influence. He has come to break his power. If he submits to the evil people will inflict on him, his is a free submission out of love for the Father and for humanity.

Before it all happens, he protests again that the ultimate cause of his consent to this death is not the prince of this world but the commandment he received from his Father, the life direction his Father gave him. He suffers to reconcile us with the Father and to manifest to us how he has become one with us in our suffering, humiliation and depression. Serene in his dedication to his divine life call, aware of his independent, free acceptance of death, Christ himself gives the sign to leave: "Come now, let us go."

"Thank you, Lord, for granting us your peace. Your peace does not consist in the absence of strife, it does not exclude dissension or tension. For you have also said: "Do not suppose that I have come to bring peace to the earth: it is not peace I have come to bring, but a sword. For I have come to set a man against his father, a daughter against her mother, a daughter-in-law against her mother-in-law. A man's enemies will be those of his own household." (Mt. 10:34-36)

"Neither is your peace an emotional feeling of contentment and security. Your peace, Jesus, is rooted in your oneness with the Father. My peace must rest in my union with you and through you with the Father. You maintained that peace of union in the midst of slander, threats, persecution, ridicule, suffering and death.

"This hidden peace of union may give rise at times to felt equanimity but that too is your gift. I often lose my equanimity when suffering strikes, and misunderstanding comes my way. Only you can grant me that inward composure that is yours. It must emerge from your parting gift. For it is one of the fruits of your peace. It is not the composure I myself can come to. The mystery of your peace exists already before me. I must try to find myself in your already existing peace; I must clothe myself with it.

"Peace in its fullness is present only in God. And you, Jesus, are the human carrier of the divine peace in this world. Your peace is not visible to the world. To share your peace I have to give up my striving for worldly satisfaction. As long as I care for the peace the world holds out, I will experience discord and dissatisfaction. Freedom from this world is the condition for true peace in you alone."

When Jesus says to us, "Peace is my gift to you," he says in another way that his gift to us is the eternal life of God himself. It is the same as when he promises us "my joy". (Jn. 15:11; 17:13) The prophets already announced him as a prince of peace. (Is. 9:6) They told that he would "command peace to the nations." (Ze. 9:10) He wants to instill his peace in our life. It is a treasure he gives to us. We may still be troubled on the surface of our life. But he wants to free us from discord in the core of our being.

In spite of dissension and strife in our everyday life, he wants us in our deepest self to believe in his presence. The world may give pleasure, success, possession, status, but never that inner assurance that he gives to us as a reflection of his presence and his love.

"You granted me the hidden state of peace with God in the core of my being. At times you allow an experience of peace to spread itself out from that core into my daily life. But I am not always ready for that gift. I have set my heart anxiously on too many things. I struggle for success. I vehemently pursue perfection. There is in my pursuits a hidden violence. I am driven by the idle hope that peace will be mine when my dreams and desires come true. But this contentment will not be the reflection of your own peace which you established in me, Jesus. It is the shallow, passing peace of the world. Make me less eager for such incidental gratifications, more longing for your peace alone."

Only his peace gives full meaning to our life. Only faith in the divine life he granted us can silence our restlessness. Let us give up our anxious cravings. Let the desire for his peace surpass all others. We should empty ourselves of all other desires. "Your attitude must be Christ's . . . he emptied himself." (Ph. 2:5-7)

Moments of worldly peace vanish like flowers that delight us with their fragrance only to wither away. What may remain is a memory that makes us feel good and sad at the same time. Sad because the passing peace of the world proved again not to be the peace we had expected it to be.

Every time we pursue worldly peace in the expectation of final contentment, we find disappointment instead. Disappointment in turn intensifies our impatient striving after a merely human peace of mind. The peace of this world is doomed to fade. The more we set our heart on it, the more we will suffer at its vanishing away.

As long as our life is filled with impatient desire, we will not find his peace. We must renounce this life of restless striving and share in his love and desire for his Father and his Kingdom—a desire that God's will be done no matter what our own wishes are. Then he will give us peace that is not ephemeral as is the peace of this world. The fruit of his peace is the fruit of a grain of wheat dying in the earth. "I solemnly assure you, unless the grain of wheat falls in the earth and dies, it remains just a grain of wheat. But if it dies, it produces much fruit." (Jn. 12:24)

Our peace should be rooted in the faith that "with his pinions the Lord will cover you, and under his wings you shall take refuge; his faithfulness is a buckler and a shield." (Ps. 91:4-5) We should die to our desire for the peace of this world, for "precious in

the eyes of the Lord is the death of his faithful ones."
(Ps. 116:15)

"Thank you, Lord, for telling me that you love me,
for assuring me that the peace of union with God is
already a reality in my life. When you allow that state
of peace to flow over in my moods and feelings, don't
let me resist your gift. One cause of my resistance may
be that I see you more as a master of affliction than a
master of peace. I am so disappointed in myself that I
punish myself by harsh condemnation. I cast you then
in my own image."

"I think thoughts of peace, and not of affliction.
You shall call upon me and I will hear you; and I will
bring back your captivity from all places." (Entrance
Song, 31st Sunday) "I am gracious and merciful, slow
to anger and of great kindness. I am good to all and
compassionate to all." (Ps. 145:8-9)

*No matter how shaken you are or how badly you
act, when you call upon me, I will hear you. I will
bring back your captivity from all places. Your
concerns are so spread out that you are closed to the
serenity I allow sometimes to flow from the state of
peace given to you.*

"Please, bring back my captivity from all places. I
feel captivated by popular movements, projects,
ambitions, overinvolvement. These concerns drive me
on relentlessly. I push people around to make my
plans come true and I am pushed around in turn. I
drop my prayers to gain time for action. I skip
moments of rest and recollection. No longer do I find

time to gently nurse my soul. I have put myself into captivity.

"Lord, still and quiet my soul, nurse it back to the life of peace as gently as a nursing mother. Arrogance is one main cause of my captivity. I take on more than I can handle. I involve myself in too many things at once. I set goals that are obviously too sublime for me. Help me to say:

"O Lord, my heart is not proud
    nor are my eyes haughty;
I busy not myself with great things,
    nor with things too sublime for me.
Nay, rather, I have stilled and quieted
    my soul like a weaned child.
Like a weaned child on its mother's lap,
    so is my soul within me."

(Ps. 131:1-3)

# EPILOGUE

# LIVING WITH THE SCRIPTURES

## EPILOGUE

## LIVING WITH THE SCRIPTURES

This meditative reading of "the last discourse" could be seen as an example of formative scripture reading.

In the last decennia there has been perhaps more interest in the scriptures among many faithful than in any century since the Reformation. Recently the popularity of scriptural studies seems to be declining. Attention has shifted to the inner life. We see a rise of interest in spirituality, in the spiritual masters, in meditation techniques and books of prayers. Not only publications about western but also about eastern spiritualities are avidly sought after.

What has happened? Do people experience a certain fatigue with the abundance of excellent exegetical commentary? Perhaps, but other explanations are possible.

The scriptures are written in a language foreign to

the contemporary mind. Their stories and sayings are imbued with a culture unfamiliar to people living today. The understanding of its texts presupposes a minimum of exegetical knowledge and theological insight. The Church, therefore, considered it its first obligation to make this minimum knowledge available to the faithful. It was like handing them over the first key to the secrets of the scripture. This key would open the outer chamber of this sanctuary. Only then would it be possible to open the door to the inner room where the treasures of spiritual meanings are hidden.

This wise concern of the Church was well responded to. Scripture scholars and writers in the field of religion popularized the exegetical and theological insights necessary for the understanding of the sacred text. Courses and seminars were offered to all who were interested. The faithful in turn responded with enthusiasm to this concerted effort to make the scriptures more available.

This enthusiasm could lead to illusion. The hiddenness of the meaning of the scriptures is due not only to unfamiliarity with the archeological, linguistic, and theological characteristics of the text. There is also a transcendent meaning which does not touch immediately the experience of the average reader, even if he is informed exegetically. He may not be ready to reach out to this deeper, spiritual significance and should be assisted in this attempt.

Exegetical and theological information—no matter how necessary—did not solve all problems of scripture reading, especially when this reading becomes meditative and formative.

Many publications and tape recordings on scripture are excellent from the viewpoint of information and explanation. They are less helpful as a witness for the living mystery of salvation contained in these sacred writings. Sometimes the speaker, writer or discussion leader in this field assumed more and more the role of a teacher. It is possible that part of the fatigue people experience in regard to exegetical publications and lectures is due to a certain one-sidedness; that is, while highly stimulated intellectually they may be starving inspirationally. Mind-knowledge is not complemented by heart knowledge; abstract information is lacking in sufficient application to daily life. This feeling of exegetical satiation may be one of the factors that led to the shift of attention to prayer experiences—a shift indicated by a change of interest in publications.

People may feel that a purely exegetical scripture reading is not enough to assist them in the inspiration and direction of their day to day spiritual life. In other words a scripture reading that is only informative may defeat its own purpose as a popular source of daily spiritual living. Every time in history that scripture reading was reduced to information that appealed mainly to a more theologically sophisticated public the popular interest in its treasures and mysteries has waned considerably.

Formative scripture reading aims at nourishing the soul; it should not merely be an exercise of the mind, for in that case the Bible becomes mainly a tool for the transfer of knowledge. One may get lost in concepts and lose contact with the transcendent richness of the text. Scripture reading may soon be experienced as something superfluous; interesting and informative—yes, but not really necessary as a source of spiritual enrichment and practice. The reader may mistakenly feel that the latter will be taken care of better, or even exclusively, by the writings of the spiritual masters and their popularizers. He may no longer turn to the scriptures themselves for this kind of nourishment.

The same problem applies to scripture texts quoted in sermons and articles when it is done in a merely informative way. They are soon experienced as rather remote information or accidental illustration that could as well be omitted or would fit better some academic course or seminar.

Bible groups too may foster a one-sided approach. Much time is spent poring over texts in search of exegetical and theological clarification. Little or no time is left for an inspirational-practical approach. The mainly intellectual approach is often appreciated by the participants on the spot, but they find little to carry over into daily life. It leaves their defenses in tact; neither does it challenge them nor arouse the initial anguish one may feel when confronted with his own opaqueness in the realm of the life of spiritual experience.

Any time the word is highlighted only in its rational and informative meaning, its formative meaning tends to be diminished or forgotten entirely. The main reason for a loss of interest in scripture reading may be that the content of this reading cannot be experienced any longer in the context of daily life; hence it may be given up easily. People ask themselves why do regular scripture reading at all if it has no relationship to daily living? They begin to wonder if informative and rational reading cannot be done better in school. The consequences of this attitude, when widespread, can be harmful to all of Christianity. Scripture reading could diminish or disappear as a formative spiritual exercise; it becomes a mainly intellectual enterprise.

Formative scripture reading can also be frustrated by a one-sided tendency to moralism. A Christian may admit that the transfer of exegetical and theological knowledge should not be the only purpose of scripture reading. He may maintain instead that scripture reading should serve right moral action. Especially militant Christians are inclined to use the Bible mainly as a source of ethical conviction. They want Bible reading to prepare Christians for the right options in service of peace and justice in society. They feel less attracted to spiritual attitudes of humility, gratefulness, inner joy, adoration, interior peace, obedience—attitudes also cultivated by the sacred texts. They may not feel at ease with these attitudes, for they cannot be translated directly into revolutionary energy and action.

It is undeniably true that the ethical inspiration of the scriptures is important; so was the information the scriptures can give us about which we spoke earlier. Yet both the informative and moral meanings of the scriptures are not the first aim of a formative spiritual reading.

## *Scripture Reading—An Exercise in Personal Religious Surface Experiences*

Experience is popular at present. Many people feel that the main meaning of meditative scripture reading is to nourish their personal religious surface experiences in prayer and daily life. They feel disappointed when the text does not respond to their own religious experiences, reinforcing and deepening them. They resent the gap between their personally felt spirituality and the objective world of symbols, prayers, parables and events presented by the scriptures.

It is evident that the scriptures have something to do with spiritual experience. There must be a connection between the speaking of the Spirit in our heart and his speaking in the scriptures. Yet we do not believe that formative scripture reading aims first of all at the representation or nourishment of the felt religious surface experiences of the reader. We will see later that formative scripture reading may evoke potential spiritual depth experiences that express profound spiritual aspirations God implanted in our spirit.

The scriptures present us objectively with the mystery of the saving Lord. They do so by means of sacred texts which have been acknowledged as inspired by the Spirit. Many of them received, moreover, an objective doctrinal explanation by the Church.

It is difficult for people today to appreciate this degree of objectivity—especially when a passage seems at odds with personal religious surface feelings they have cherished for a long time. Yet this objectivity is characteristic of the scriptures; it elevates their content beyond subjective surface experiences. The spiritual reader may initially experience inner resistance when he tries to enter wholeheartedly into this objective content.

In meditative scripture reading something formative happens to the reader. The reader takes up the text but after that initial action on his part, he is less and less the initiator and more and more the responder. To be sure both elements are necessary, namely human cooperation and divine initiative. Formative scripture reading is precisely a spiritual exercise in which a divine-human interaction takes place. It is within the spiritual act of the reader that also a divine acting is going on. The divine act of enlightenment by the text needs the human act of spiritual reading to be able to effect this textual enlightenment. This does not mean that this divine enlightenment of the reader is in any way conditioned by the human act. Divine illumination transcends at any moment the human act of the reader. Nevertheless the divine act expresses itself within the ambience of this spiritual exercise and may evoke potential spiritual depth experiences in the reader.

*Formative Scripture Reading as Celebration of the Mystery of Salvation*

The text of Holy Scripture is first of all an objective presentation inspired by the Holy Spirit and guaranteed and safeguarded by the Church. This objective text—when approached meditatively—gives rise to a subjective integration by the reader. The latter implies the actualization of a potentiality for deeper spiritual self experience. Formative scripture reading is a dialectical exercise; it implies a dialogue between what is pre-given objectively in the text and subjective life experience of the reader. In formative scripture reading we receive all from the text and yet we re-create it personally in terms of our life experience.

What is objectively pre-given in the scriptures are the mysteries of the God of salvation and of the historical Christ: his life, suffering, death and resurrection. We did not invent these historical occurrences; they are facts handed over to us. Hence such attitudes as receptivity, docility, respectful listening, prayerful openness and acceptance are necessary in any meditative scripture reading. It is the attitude of faith. Meditative scripture reading, without the believing acceptance of the reality of these mysteries, would be nothing more than noble self-expression. It may have educational and at times therapeutic effects. But reflective reading of Holy Scripture in this sense does not differ from the techniques of a merely human spirituality that can be found also outside Christianity. Such reading without faith may foster a humanistic spiritual formation but not a spiritual formation in Christ.

This objective character of a Christian reading of Holy Scripture has great consequences for the practice of this spiritual exercise. The attitude of the formative scripture reader cannot be one of merely introspective self presence. The Christian reader should not be fixated on his own inner center. Scripture reading is not self-analysis. One condition for formative scripture reading is de-centering in the sense of relativizing the ego-self. Some One else becomes central: Christ, his person, life, words, and deeds and the preparation for his coming in the Hebrew scriptures. The Christian scripture reader should allow his vision to be elevated to something that surpasses the present moment and his personal surface experiences, problems and interests. Such transcendence presupposes moments of stillness, prayerful pauses that are necessary during the reading.

A second consequence of this objective character of the scriptures is the importance of an objective look at the fundamental meanings and structures of the text. The reader should acquaint himself first with the basic doctrinal and exegetical information necessary for an understanding of the fundamental content of the text. A kind of pre-meditative reading of prefaces, introductions, commentaries, footnotes and other relevant literature should serve as a remote

preparation for the meditative reading proper. A
proximate preparation is the recollection of one's soul
before God in the prayerful hope that grace will
establish in us the receptivity necessary for the
reading.

The knowledge to be gathered during the remote
preparation may restrict itself to the minimum
necessary to avoid doctrinal error or gross linguistic
misunderstanding. A scripture course, if available,
could be of considerable help but is not absolutely
necessary provided the right literature can be found.

It is crucial to keep some distinction between the
pre-meditative and the meditative exercise, between
informative and formative reading. Not an absolute
separation but only a distinction is required. During
informative reading the objective doctrinal and
exegetical meaning is in the foreground of our
attention. In the background are the inspirational-
practical meanings the Spirit may communicate to us
to foster our unique formation in Christ. In turn,
during formative reading, information lingers in the
background while the formative influence of the Spirit
is the center of our waiting attention.

The proximate preparation for formative scripture
reading consists in the creation of conditions which
facilitate inner gentleness, quiet and receptivity.
Without these attitudes it is almost impossible to be
meditatively present to the text. If we are not at rest
inwardly, we can hear only our own self, not the Spirit
speaking in the scriptures.

To make this attitude of recollected listening

possible, it may be necessary to engage at other times in concentration exercises. One should try to develop the art of relativizing the busy ego self. This exercise can help the reader to lose excessive self-centeredness and to center his whole being on the holy text he is faced with.

## Subjective Assimilation of the Scripture Text

Formative scripture reading is not merely a becoming acquainted with the objective words printed in my Bible. This reading is also subjective assimilation; it is creative and in some measure a self-expression of the reader. The reader should try in a relaxed way to recognize himself in the text, to participate as this unique person in its living truth. We must put ourselves in the text, as it were. Within the objective data of the text, we must look for moments of affinity between the text and our life experience here and now. Such moments of affinity differ, of course, from person to person. Even within the same person different periods of life and experience may give rise to different moments of affinity. Once I experience in a passage of scripture such affinity, I should abide with it, absorbing as much richness as I can take from it at this stage of my life. Passages that do not evoke this affinity ought to be passed over quickly, whereas texts that do stand out should be dwelt upon longer.

The main condition for my being influenced formatively by scripture reading is that I can find my whole self back in the text. I must see in scripture a prefiguration of my own deepest thoughts, hopes, desires and feelings. My deepest experiences are often hidden from me. I cannot easily talk about them. Often I cannot formulate them at all. I may rarely think about the most fundamental aspirations God created in me as a spiritual person. I may resent their presence and resist their awareness. They may seldom come up in conversation, but when I see them in the symbols, stories and events of scripture, I may recognize myself in them—not my surface self but my deepest self—and I may then enter into the text wholeheartedly.

## The Concreteness of the Scripture Texts

The scriptures are not collections of scholarly speculations, abstract theories, or scientific treatises. They are filled with striking images, poetic prayers, lively stories and the wisdom of graced experience over the ages. Formative reading is not a "head trip". The scriptures are bound to the human heart and body.

The events, images and stories of scripture are pointers. They refer to what is invisible. To be sure, they start from what can be seen and heard, yet they are meant to be suggestion, direction, symbol, evocation. A main condition for formative scripture reading is to read more than the literal text, to see further than the story, to taste more than the first moving impression. Scripture calls us out of our limited horizon of everydayness to wider horizons. It refers us first of all to cosmos and nature; secondly to the direction of our whole self in all its dimensions; thirdly to the deepest directions of our supra-consciousness to which the symbols and stories of scripture give a concrete form; finally to the historical events of God's guidance of the chosen people and of the life, teaching, suffering, death and resurrection of our Lord.

*Relation of Scripture to Our Experience of Cosmos and Nature*

Many scripture texts, for example, those of the Psalms and of the parables of the Gospel refer to nature, to mountains and valleys, stars and oceans, fire and water, fields and flowers, snow and ice, wind and rain, seeds and trees, sowing and harvesting. Others refer to the rhythms we experience in nature: day and night, light and darkness, spring, summer, autumn and winter.

The message of the scriptures goes beyond this reminder of our cosmic experiences on the vital level; yet this message is not totally unrelated to these experiences. Man is also a vital participant in nature, a creature among creatures. The formative function of scripture is to integrate also the vital self dimension into the mystery of divine liberation. Cosmos and nature correspond to this vital self dimension. Together with this basic human experience they become integrated into this same mystery.

Many passages, moreover, express other vital

human needs and experiences, even when sublimated. They speak about eating and drinking, falling and rising, thirst and tiredness, marrying and falling in love, sensuality, sickness and dying, weeping and rejoicing. They highlight the vital situation of man. The human person as already formed by vital experiences can find himself back in the scriptures.

## Scripture and the Functional Self Dimension

The functioning of the human person is depicted in numerous Biblical events and stories, in New Testament parables and comparisons, in the life of Jesus and his disciples. Man is invited to dominate and subject the earth, to function as God's steward in an effective and masterful way. In the Gospel he is called upon to express the love of God and to foster the Kingdom effectively by functioning concretely in this world, using his talents and not burying them.

The functional self dimension is integrated in the total meaning of the scripture text. The reader is reminded of the functional roles, duties, needs, and ambitions he experiences in his daily life. His culture has already formed his functional life. Scripture helps him to integrate this functional formation into his spiritual formation.

## Scripture and the Spiritual Self Dimension

We are not only pneumatic persons guided by the Holy Spirit who is given to us. The Holy Spirit, or

Pneuma in St. Paul's terminology, permeates and elevates our natural human spirit. The human spirit is the deepest dimension of the self.

Our spirit self contains our deepest aspirations. Many scripture texts symbolize these aspirations. They offer a mirror of our deepest interiority. We have usually no clear awareness of what is alive in our supra-consciousness: a natural faith, hope and love; spiritual convictions, ideals and aspirations; a potential contemplative presence. These spiritual tendencies may enter our pre-consciousness and consciousness as concrete images, concepts, feelings, as longings for total freedom and salvation, for the fullness of peace, love, security, for paradise here on earth. These spirit-inspired images represent the nobility of the human being, the most sublime dimension of his nature.

Such inspired images find their representations in art and natural religion, in literature, music, painting, architecture, sculpture, drama, ballet and films. Their deepest expression is found in the "stories" of religions.

The reader can recognize this profound and most hidden aspect of himself in the scriptures. Initially he may experience scriptural symbols as something he is vaguely attuned to once in a while without being well aware of this affinity between his spirit self and the text.

The scripture text awakens the reader to his own interiority. He begins to recognize himself as spirit self. For example, the setting and sphere of the last discourse plays upon spiritual aspirations, intuitions, and feelings of the reader, even if he is not, or not yet, a Christian. The gathering of disciples around a beloved master who has to leave them, the intimacy of a festive meal with friends who are like brothers, the last moving words, the drama of betrayal by a friend, the seriousness and fear evoked by the fast approaching reality of suffering and death, the leave-taking of the Beloved One—all these events can evoke deeply personal-spiritual experiences. Such experiences find a concrete portrayal in this discourse. Any serious and open reader—Christian or non-Christian—recognizes in them his own latent spiritual experiences and the core dimension of spirit they imply. He is touched by them. Some of these things he may have experienced in some measure in himself or in others. Or he senses that such things can happen also to him and may move his spirit similarly.

It is precisely these experiences that should be fostered and valued in formative scripture reading. No person who reads mindfully the Passion and Death of Jesus can remain unmoved by this suffering of an innocent man, his dread of death, his struggle to accept his "fate," the maliciousness of people who make others suffer and yet do not know what they are doing, the ridicule of the idealist who perishes as a loser while mediocre functionaries live on, esteemed by their fellow men as wise and balanced leaders; the harshness of human justice, leading to punishment of the innocent while unjust people are not hindered or condemned; being left alone by all of one's friends and almost, it seems, by God. Any reader who lives some minimum of self presence can certainly recognize himself in this portrayal.

Or think about the event of the resurrection: the experience of the paradox of life and death. Out of death, life springs forth. This aspiration for life through death expresses the supra-conscious spiritual aspiration for lasting life, for rebirth, for paradise, for a future of pure joy and peace.

The hidden aspirations of the human spirit have found form in such conscious and pre-conscious aspirations. The latter find their concrete expression among others in the symbols and stories of scripture.

The final formation of the whole human self by the Holy Spirit complements, integrates, and harmonizes not only the natural and cultural formation of the vital and functional self dimensions but also the formation of the human spiritual dimension.

Formative scripture reading is one spiritual exercise used by the Holy Spirit to effect this graced formation of the person as a whole. This self recognition is a meeting of spiritual experience and its exteriorization in the scriptures—a meeting crucial for the formative impact of this reading. I must see myself mirrored in the scriptures: I must realize it is all about me!

*Formative Scripture Reading as Participation in Sacred History*

Formative scripture reading is also meditative presence to the past and what happened there with the chosen people and later with Christ and his disciples.

Scripture offers infinitely more than events, images, prayers and stories, in which the human person can recognize himself in his vital, functional, and spiritual dimensions. If this were the only effect of scripture reading, it could perhaps be nothing more than the projection of the reader's hopes and dreams on the screen of the scriptures—a self-centered looking at his own mirrored image. Formative scripture reading would be merely an exercise in the heightening of self awareness. Such self awareness is necessary but if increased awareness of self would be the only effect of scripture reading, it would leave the reader still more dissatisfied than before. Aspirations which remain unfulfilled are more difficult to live with when they are made conscious than when they stay unnoticed in the spiritual supra-conscious of the person.

The reader, therefore, must be receptive to the Holy Spirit who speaks both in the scriptures and in his own spirit. He must be prayerfully present in faith to the historical reality of God's self communication to man in the events, stories and words of the scriptures. He must allow the Holy Spirit to transform his whole humanity through this historical truth.

Formative scripture reading is thus not simply a participation in a noble and fascinating story, nor a recognition of one's own humanity in that story. I must recognize that the content of the scriptures is not only relevant to my aspirations but contains also a real historical response to these aspirations. I must enter with my whole being into that divine response to my hidden aspirations with all the faith, hope and love the Spirit himself infuses in my spirit, elevating my natural faith, hope and love. While reading, I should maintain an attitude of prayer for increase in infused "living faith, hope and love."

Formative scripture reading is, above all, a prayerful presence to the historical Jesus. The mysteries of his life express the deepest meaning of our innate spiritual aspirations. In such reading we may experience at moments the coinciding of formative self awareness and formative Christ awareness.

My innate spiritual aspirations are lived through by Jesus. They find in him their highest possible fulfillment and expression. The Holy Spirit enables my spirit to come to a Christian self recognition while reading the scriptures. I recognize myself with all my pre-formed aspirations as being transformed in the Christ of the scriptures. I discover Christ in me and me in Christ.

Formative scripture reading without infused faith, hope and love is nothing more than a psycho-spiritual participation in a written drama of human experience. It may give rise to deepened self awareness and to some liberation of the human self; it may serve humanistic self formation; it can never foster our ultimate formation in Jesus. In that ultimate formation, Jesus becomes the form of our life in a unique way which is consonant with the essential pre-formations of our human self insofar as they are willed by his Father.

Essential for formative scripture reading is thus

that I find my whole self back in the text. The reader must be attentive both to himself and to Christ. Both kinds of attention should at a certain moment fertilize each other. That moment of formative cross-fertilization is crucial for formative scripture reading. Without it no Christian self formation takes place. What may happen is only humanistic self formation or a mere increase in abstract theological or exegetical information. All of these are praiseworthy fruits but not the most precious one that only a Christian formative reading could give rise to. The latter may be used by the Spirit to form the self in Christ himself: Jesus encounters the concrete person and the living person encounters Jesus.

## Scripture Reading and Reading in Systematic Theology

The richer the intellectual background of a Christian, the more necessary theological sophistication becomes for him. To transform all of his life in Christ implies for him also the transformation of his secular knowledge. Such transformation of knowledge is impossible without contemporary theological sophistication. Systematic theology can help him understand how to integrate intellectually the insights and findings of the arts and sciences with an advancing understanding of the Revelation.

Yet this intellectual integration, no matter how basic and necessary, is not enough. This theologically enlightened secular knowledge has to be integrated in turn into the life of the whole person. Otherwise, it cannot foster his unique self formation in Christ; it would remain in him as a worthwhile yet foreign body not assimilated into the living totality of his emergent self in and with Jesus.

This formative assimilation is fostered by fidelity to fundamental spiritual exercises. They have been tried out and described by the great spiritual masters over the centuries. One of them is meditative scripture reading. The new religious discipline of formative spirituality tries among other things to find the unifying essence of the countless descriptions presented by the masters, meanwhile taking into account the state of present-day knowledge and experience.

Readings in systematic theology can be done formatively. Yet the primary aim of systematic theology is not the immediate formation of each unique human self in its spiritual-emotional totality. Moreover, the main medium of systematic theological speculation is the language of abstract concepts. This language does not direct itself primarily to the concrete living self as a whole. Systematic theology directs itself, first of all, to the faith-enlightened intellect of the reader. This fact makes the text of systematic theology a less appropriate medium for formative spiritual reading. Systematic theological writings can be used that way, but the reader would have to engage in much translation of intellectual speculation into terms of concrete living, terms that are directly relevant to his daily personal spiritual life and problems. Not all people would be as able to make this translation effectively. A special difficulty would be the necessity during theological reading to shift repeatedly from an abstract intellectual approach to a concrete, intuitive-personal approach.

More immediately formative are the scriptures and those concrete, inspirational writings of the spiritual masters that do not contain the theoretical considerations of the latter about the spiritual life.

The scriptures are filled with concrete images, moving life stories, human drama, emotional expressions, wisdom of everyday living. Their efficacy for self formation surpasses that of conceptual information by means of abstract language. The reason is that life knowledge precedes conceptual knowledge. For example, we have first the concrete experience of felt relief when somebody takes a heavy package from us or when we see or read about this event as described in concrete experiential terms. Only then do we form the abstract concept "relief." After that, we may develop the transcendent concept of "relief" as a liberation of all that burdens the self in this life.

Not only do experiential images precede our concepts, they also have a primary and powerful formative influence on the human self. The life stories, symbols and imagery of the scriptures do not appeal to only one modality of the human self: the intellect. They appeal to the whole self, to the spiritual, functional and vital self dimensions and all their articulations, and to all modalities of presence: spirit, mind, heart, memory, imagination and sensate presence.

This explains that not only the scriptures but also the sacred writings of other religions, arts, literature and poetic philosophies use life stories, imageries and symbols. In regard to this aspect of formative use, there is no difference between them and the scriptures.

Concrete wisdom, imagery, and symbolism have a formative influence on the person as a whole provided that he makes himself totally present to the scriptures. This means that the reader should not reduce himself to a one-sided intellectual stand or to a one-sided sentimental presence. He should be present to the text with a certain sensitivity which enables him to understand and experience the symbols and images of the scriptures. The cultivation of a rich and refined sensibility is of great help to the reader. Any voluntary or unconscious deformation of his sensibility makes the reader less receptive to the imagery of the scriptures.

This means that the formation of human sensibility is a remote but necessary preparation for meditative scripture reading. In many cases, it may be necessary to provide Christians with pre-meditative exercises, readings and presentations which complement the lack of formation of their human sensibility. This need also implies the development of sensitivity for tradition and culture. A rich, human sensibility requires, above all, a wide range of value experiences.

Without them, scripture reading could remain sterile.

Lack of sensibility is often the cause of the inability of the reader to participate effectively in formative scripture reading. He does not have the sensitivity necessary for the experience of deeply human values which surpass the surface needs of the self. Again, this lack of depth does not necessarily indicate a cultural or intellectual poverty but an insufficient development of human sensitivity. Often true sensitivity for human values is clearly present in many uneducated people; sometimes it cannot be found in scholars and intellectuals.

We should realize that wisdom of living, images and symbols operate differently than concepts. This is also true of the duration they need to penetrate formatively into the human self. Concepts are understood or not understood; by themselves they have no further formative penetration. Images and symbols are often not immediately understood in their fullness. Only part of their truth is revealed to the reader. They tend, however, to sink deeply in the pre-conscious and supra-conscious of the person. By repetition they gradually communicate their treasures to the reader, slowly transforming his life.

Scriptural images and symbols influence us usually unconsciously and slowly, but most profoundly. Many years later, they may still radiate their influence like atomic material that is deeply buried under the ground but still radiates its power invisibly. They work through reminiscence. It may be that the image of

Jesus at the last supper does not mean much to us at this moment. But if this image is experienced in some measure, it can have a great formative influence later in life. The person may experience something similar to what our Lord experienced at the last supper. He may suddenly remember what he read at that time and say to himself: now I understand more deeply what it meant for Jesus and what it should mean for me. No scripture image can reveal to us at once all the richness of its content: the last discourse, for example, can tell us every day something different and something new. The same is true of a great work of art like a sonata of Beethoven or a painting by Rembrandt. The process of formation by scripture reading is thus very different from what one experiences in a conceptual transfer of knowledge.

Formative scripture reading demands much patience. Not only God has his time but also the scriptural symbols and images need time to unfold their formative power in the soul.

The formative scripture reader should realize that he can only keep in mind and heart what touched him deeply. What was learned only conceptually is fast forgotten. It is true that faith begins with hearing and learning. Yet faith becomes only formative if this learning was a graced appropriation which finds a reverberation in the depths of the self, a reverberation which is not so much rational or intellectual but intuitive-spiritual.

## REFERENCES

van Kaam, Adrian. Scripture and Spirituality. Ch. IV, pp. 82-107 in: *In Search of Spiritual Identity.* Denville, NJ: Dimension Books, 1975.

_____Spiritual Reading as Common Direction. Ch. XIII, pp. 345-366 in: *The Dynamics of Spiritual Self Direction.* Denville, N.J.: Dimension Books, 1976.

_____Formative Scripture Reading. Epilogue pp. 125-152 in: *The Woman at the Well.* Denville, N.J.: Dimension Books, 1976.